THE LOVE AFFAIRS OF AN OLD MAID

LILIAN BELL

1st WORLD
LIBRARY
Literary Society

The Love Affairs of an Old Maid

Lilian Bell

© 1st World Library, 2008
PO Box 2211
Fairfield, IA 52556
www.1stworldlibrary.com
First Edition

LCCN: 2007935399

Softcover ISBN: 978-1-4218-9351-8
Hardcover ISBN: 978-1-4218-9451-5
eBook ISBN: 978-1-4218-9251-1

Purchase *"The Love Affairs of an Old Maid"*
as a traditional bound book at:
www.1stWorldLibrary.com/purchase.asp?ISBN=978-1-4218-9351-8

1st World Library is a literary, educational organization
dedicated to:

- Creating a free internet library of downloadable ebooks

- Hosting writing competitions and offering book publishing
  scholarships.

Interested in more 1st World Library books? contact:
literacy@1stworldlibrary.com

Check us out at: www.1stworldlibrary.com

1st World Library Literary Society

Giving Back to the World

"If you want to work on the core problem, it's early school literacy."

- James Barksdale, former CEO of Netscape

"No skill is more crucial to the future of a child, or to a democratic and prosperous society, than literacy."

- Los Angeles Times

"Literacy... means far more than learning how to read and write... The aim is to transmit... knowledge and promote social participation."

- UNESCO

"Literacy is not a luxury, it is a right and a responsibility. If our world is to meet the challenges of the twenty-first century we must harness the energy and creativity of all our citizens."

- President Bill Clinton

"Parents should be encouraged to read to their children, and teachers should be equipped with all available techniques for teaching literacy, so the varying needs and capacities of individual kids can be taken into account."

- Hugh Mackay

"Some ships reach happy ports that are not steered"

DEDICATION

This book is dedicated very fondly to my beloved family, who, in their anxiety to render me material assistance, have offered me such diverse opinions as to its merit that their criticisms radiate from me in as many directions as there are spokes to a wheel.

This leaves the distraught hub with no opinion of its own, and with flaring, ragged edges.

Nevertheless, thus must it appear before the public, whose opinion will be the tire which shall enable my wheel to revolve. If it be favorable, one may look for smooth riding; if unfavorable, one must expect jolts.

PREFACE

It is a pity that there is no prettier term to bestow upon a girl bachelor of any age than Old Maid. "Spinster" is equally uncomfortable, suggesting, as it does, corkscrew curls and immoderate attenuation of frame; while "maiden lady," which the ultra-punctilious substitute, is entirely too mincing for sensible, whole-souled people to countenance.

I dare say that more women would have the courage to remain unmarried were there so euphonious a title awaiting them as that of "bachelor," which, when shorn of its accompanying adjective "old," simply means unmarried.

The word "bachelor," too, has somewhat of a jaunty sound, implying to the sensitive ear that its owner could have been married—oh, several times over—if he had wished. But both "spinster" and "old maid" have narrow, restricted attributes, which, to say the least, imply doubt as to past opportunity.

Names are covertly responsible for many overt acts. Carlyle, when he said, "The name is the earliest garment you wrap around the earth-visiting me. Names? Not only all common speech, but Science, Poetry itself, if thou consider it, is no other than a right naming," sounded a wonderful note in Moral Philosophy, which rings false many a time in real life, when to ring true would change the whole face of affairs.

Lilian Bell

Thus I boldly affirm, that were there a proper sounding title to cover the class of unmarried women, many a marriage which now takes place, with either moderate success or distinct failure, would remain in pleasing embryo.

Of the three evils among names for my book, therefore, I leave you to determine whether I have chosen the greatest or least. The writing of it came about in this way.

In a conversation concerning modern marriage, the unwisdom people display in choice, and the complicated affair it has come to be from a pastoral beginning, I said lightly, "I shall write a book upon this subject some fine day, and I shall call it 'The Love Affairs of an Old Maid,' because popular prejudice decrees that the love affairs of an old maid necessarily are those of other people."

No sooner had the name suggested in broad jest taken form in my mind than straightway every thought I possessed crystallized around it, and I found myself impelled by a malevolent Fate to begin it.

It became a fixed intention on a Sunday morning in church during a most excellent sermon, the text and substance of which I have forgotten. Doubtless more of real worth and benefit to mankind was pent up in that sermon than four books of my own writing could accomplish. But, with the delightful candor of John Kendrick Bangs, I explain my lapse of memory thus—

> "I dote on Milton and on Robert Burns;
> I love old Marryat—his tales of pelf;
> I live on Byron; but my heart most yearns
> Towards those sweet things that I've penned myself."

So the book has been written. The existence of the Old Maid

often has been a precarious one; she has been surrounded by danger, once narrowly escaping cremation. But my humanity towards dumb brutes saved her. I might have sacrificed a woman, but I could not kill a cat. So she lives, unconsciously owing her life to her cat.

Thus she comes to you, bearing her friends in her heart. I should scarcely dare ask you to welcome her, did I not suspect that her friends are yours. You have your Flossy and your Charlie Hardy without doubt. Pray Heaven you have a Rachel to outweigh them.

CHICAGO, *March, 1893*.

CONTENTS

I

I INTRODUCE ME TO MYSELF

"There is a luxury in self-dispraise;
And inward self-disparagement affords
To meditative spleen a grateful feast."

To-morrow I shall be an Old Maid. What a trying thing to have to say even to one's self, and how vexed I should be if anybody else said it to me! Nevertheless, it is a comfort to be brutally honest once in a while to myself. I do not dare, I do not care, to be so to everybody. But with my own self, I can feel that it is strictly a family affair. If I hurt my feelings, I can grieve over it until I apologize. If I flatter myself, I am only doing what every other woman in the world is doing in her innermost consciousness, and flattery as honest as flattery from one's own self naturally would be could not fail to please me. Besides, it would have the unique value of being believed by both sides—a situation in the flattery line which I fancy has no rival.

It is well to become acquainted with one's self at all hazards, and as I am going to be my own partner in the rubber of life, I can do nothing better than to study my own hand. So, to harrow up my feelings as only I dare to do, I write down that it is really true of me that I passed the first corner five years ago, and to-morrow I shall be 30.

What a disagreeable figure a 3 is; I never noticed it before. It looks so self-satisfied. And as to that fat, hollow 0 which follows it—I always did detest round numbers.

30; there it goes again. I must accustom myself to it privately, so I write it down once more, and it laughs in my face and mocks me. Then I laugh back at it and say aloud that it is true, and for the time being I have cowed it and become its master. What boots it if the laughter is a trifle hollow? There is no harm in deceiving two miserable little figures.

Let me revel in my youth while I may. To-night I am a gay young thing of twenty-nine. To-morrow I shall be an Old Maid. I have very little time left in which to make myself ridiculous and have it excused on account of my youth. But somehow I do not feel very gay. I have a curious feeling about my heart, as if I were at a burial—one where I was burying something that I had always loved very dearly, but secretly, and which would always be a sweet and tender memory with me. I feel nervous, too, quite as if I did not know whether to laugh or to cry. I remember that Alice Asbury said she was hysterical just before she was married. I wonder if a woman's feelings on the eve of being an Old Maid are unlike those of one about to become a bride.

My cat sits eying me with sleepy approval. I always liked cats. And tea. Why have I never thought of it before? It is not my fault that I am an Old Maid. I was cut out for one. All my tendencies point that way. Please don't blame me, good people. Come here, Tabby. You and Missis will grow old together.

After all, it is a sad thing when one realizes for the first time that one's youth is slipping away. But why? Why do women of great intelligence, of intellect even, blush with pleasure at the implication of youth?

There are fashions in thought as well as in dress, and the best of us follow both, as sheep follow their leader. We will sometimes follow our neighbor's line of insular prejudice, when worlds could not bribe us to copy her grammar or her gowns. Dull people admire youth. They excuse its follies; they adore its prettiness. That it is only a period of education, and that real life begins with maturity, does not enter into their minds. The odor of bread and butter does not nauseate them. Dull people, I say—and God pity us, most of us are dull—admire youth. Men love it. Therefore we all want to be young. We strive to be young, nay, we *will* be young.

I am no better than my neighbors. I, too, am young when I am with people. But there are times when I am alone when the strain of being young relaxes, and I luxuriate in being old, old, old, when I cease being contemporary, and look back fondly to the time when the world and I were in embryo.

And yet I wonder if extreme age is as repulsive to everybody as it is to me. Forty seems a long way off. I fancy people at forty become very uninteresting to the oncoming generation. Fifty is grandmotherly and suitable for little else. Sixty, seventy, and beyond seem to me one horrible jumble of wrinkles and wheezes and false beauty and general unpleasantness. Oh, I hope, if I should live to be over fifty, that I may be a pleasant old person. I hope my teeth will fit me, and the parting to my wave be always in the middle. I hope my fingers will always come fully to the ends of my gloves, and that I never shall wear my spectacles on top of my head. But I hope more than all that it isn't wicked to wish to die before I come to these things.

Before I entirely lose my youth—in other words, before I become an Old Maid, let me see what I must give up. Lovers, of course. That goes without saying. And if I give them up, it will not do to have their photographs standing around. They must be—oh! and their letters—must they too be destroyed? Dear me, no! I'll just fold them all together and lay them away, like a wedding-dress which never has been worn. And I'll put girls' pictures or missionaries' or martyrs' into the empty frames. Martyrs' would be most appropriate.

Now for a box to put them in. A pretty box, so that one who runs may read? Not so, you sentimental Elderly Person. Take this tin box with a lock on it. There you are, done up in a japanned box and padlocked. I would say that it looks like a little coffin if I wasn't afraid of what my Alter Ego would say. She seems cross to-night. I wonder what is the matter with her. She must be getting old. I should like to hang the key around my neck on a blue ribbon, but I am afraid. "What if you should be run over and killed," she says, "or should faint away in church? Remember that you are an Old Maid." How disagreeable old maids can be! And I've got to live with this one always. I'll put the key in my purse. Nice, sensible, prosaic place, a purse.

How late it grows! I have only a little time left. I believe that clock is fast. Dear, dear! Do I want to just sit still and watch myself turn? I meant to have old age overtake me in my sleep. I think I'll stop that clock and let my youth fade from me unawares.

II

I COME INTO MY KINGDOM

"There is no compensation for the woman who feels that the chief   relation of her life has been no more than a mistake. She has lost   her crown. The deepest secret of human blessedness has half   whispered itself to her and then forever passed her by."

I have become an Old Maid, and really it is a relief. I feel as if I had left myself behind me, and that now I have a right to the interests of other people when they are freely offered. My friends always have confided in me. I suppose it is because I am receptive. Men tell me their old love affairs. Girls tell me the whole story of their engagements—how they came to take this man, and why they did not take that one. And even the most ordinary are vitally interesting. Before I know it, I am rent with the same despair which agitates the lover confiding in me; or I am wreathed in the smiles of the engaged girl who is getting her absorbing secret comfortably off her mind. It seems to comfort them to air their emotion, and sometimes I am convinced that they leave the most of it with me.

Now I can feel at liberty to enjoy and sympathize as I will.

Well, the love affairs of other people are the rightful inheritance of old maids. In sharing them I am only coming into my kingdom.

Alice Asbury has made shipwreck of hers. The girl is actively miserable and her husband is indifferently uncomfortable, which is the habit this married couple have of experiencing the same emotion.

Alice is a mass of contradictions to those who do not understand her—now in the clouds, now in the depths. Bad weather depresses her; so does a sad story, the death of a kitten, solemn music. She is correspondingly volatile in the opposite direction and often laughs at real calamities with wonderful courage. She has a fund of romance in her nature which has led her to the pass she now is in. She is clever, too, at introspection and analysis—of herself chiefly. She studies her own sensations and dissects her moods. Her selfishness is of the peculiar sort which should have kept her from marrying until she found the hundredth man who could appreciate her genius and bend it into nobler channels. Unfortunately she married one of the ninety-nine. She is not, perhaps, more selfish than many another woman, but her selfishness is different. She is mentally cross-eyed from turning her eyes inward so constantly.

She became engaged to Brandt—a man in every way worthy of her—and they loved each other devotedly. Then during a quarrel she broke the engagement, and he, being piqued by her withdrawal, immediately married May Lawrence, who had been patiently in love with him for five years, and who was only waiting for some such turn as this to deliver him into her hands. A poetic justice visits him with misery, for he still cares for Alice. May, however, is not conscious of this fact as yet.

Lilian Bell

Alice, being doubly stung by his defection, was just in the mood to do something desperate, when she began to see a great deal of Asbury, fresh from being jilted by Sallie Cox. Asbury was moody, and confided in Alice. Alice was foolish, and confided in him. They both decided that their hearts were ashes, love burned out, and life a howling wilderness, and then proceeded to exchange these empty hearts of theirs, and to go through the howling wilderness together.

Alice came to tell me about it. They had no love to give each other, she said sadly, but they were going to be married. I would have laughed at her if she had not been so tragic. But there is something about Alice, in spite of her romantic folly, (which she has adapted from the French to suit her American needs,) which forbids ridicule. Nevertheless I felt, with one of those sudden flashes of intuition, that this choice of hers was a hideous mistake. The situation repelled me. But the very strangeness of it seemed to attract the morbid Alice. And it was this one curious strain of unexplained foolishness marring her otherwise strong and in many ways beautiful character which prevented my loving her completely and safely. Nevertheless, I cared for her enough to enter my feeble and futile protest; but it was waved aside with the superb effrontery of a woman who feels that she controls the situation with her head, and whose heart is not at liberty to make uncomfortable complications. I would rather argue with a woman who is desperately in love, to prevent her marrying the man of her choice, than to try to dissuade a woman from marrying a man she has set her head upon. You feel sympathy with the former, and you have human nature and the whole glorious love-making Past at your back, to give you confidence and eloquence. But with the latter you are cowed and beaten beforehand, and tongue-tied during the contest.

So she became Alice Asbury, and these two blighted beings took a flat. Before they had been at home from their honeymoon a week she came down to see me, and told me that she hated Asbury.

Imagine a bride whose bouquet, only a month before, you had held at the altar, and heard her promise to love, honor, and obey a man until death did them part, coming to you with a confession like that. Still, if but one half she tells me of him is true, I do not wonder that she hates him.

With her revolutionary, anarchistic completeness, she has renounced the idea of compromise or adaptability as finally as if she had seen and passed the end of the world. There is no more pliability in her with regard to Asbury than there is in a steel rod. How different she used to be with Brandt! How she consulted his wishes and accommodated herself to him!

When a woman born to be ruled by love only passes by her master spirit, she becomes an anomaly in woman—she makes complications over which the psychologist wastes midnight oil, and if he never discovers the solution, it is because of its very simplicity.

All the sweetness seems to have left Alice's nature. She keeps somebody with her every moment. That one guest chamber in her flat has been occupied by all the girls that she can persuade to visit her. Asbury dislikes company, but she says she does not care. She cannot keep visitors long, because as soon as they discover that they are unwelcome to Asbury, naturally they go home.

Fortunately, Asbury does not care for Sallie Cox any more. When his vanity was wounded, his love died instantly. I think he is more in love with himself than he ever was with any woman. There are men, you know, whose one grand passion in life is for themselves. But Alice knows that Brandt still cares for her, and she feeds her romantic fancy on this fact, and has her introspective miseries to her heart's content. She is far too cool-headed a woman to do anything rash. Sometimes I think her morbid nature obtains more real satisfaction out of her joyless situation than positive happiness would compensate her for. She appears to take a certain negative pleasure in it. Their marriage is the product of a false civilization, and I pity them—at a distance—from the bottom of my heart. I am sorry for Brandt, too, for he honestly loved Alice and might have proved the hundredth man—who knows?

I do not quite know whether to be sorry for May Brandt or not, for she made complications and made them purposely. She made them so promptly, too, that she precluded the possibility of a reconciliation between Alice and Brandt. If Brandt had remained single, I doubt whether Alice would have had the courage to form an engagement with any other man. She loved him too truly to take the first step towards an eternal separation. Women seldom dare make that first move, except as a decoy. They are naturally superstitious, and even when curiously free from this trait in everything else, they cling to a little in love, and dare not tempt Fate too insolently.

A woman who has quarrelled with her lover, in her secret heart expects him back daily and hourly, no matter what the cause of the estrangement, until he becomes involved with another woman. Then she lays all the blame of his defection at the door of the alien, where, in the opinion of an Old Maid, it generally belongs.

If other women would let men alone, constancy would be less of a hollow mockery. (Query, but is it constancy where there is no temptation to be fickle?) Nevertheless, let "another woman" sympathize with an estranged lover, and place a little delicate blame upon his sweetheart and flatter him a great deal, and *presto!* you have one of those criss-cross engagements which turns life to a dull gray for the aching heart which is left out.

If, too, when this honestly loving woman appears to take the first step, her actions and mental processes could be analyzed and timed, it frequently would prove that, with her quicker calculations, she foresaw the fatal effect of the "other-woman" element, and, desirous of protecting her vanity, reached blindly out to the nearest man at her command, and married him with magnificent effrontery, just to circumvent humiliation and to take a little wind out of the other woman's sails. But could you make her lover believe that? Never.

And so May Lawrence played the "other woman" in the Asbury tragedy. I wonder if she is satisfied with her role. A girl who wilfully catches a man's heart on the rebound, does the thing which involves more risk than anything else malevolent fate could devise.

On the whole, I think I am sorry for her, for she has apples of Sodom in her hand, although as yet to her delighted gaze they appear the fairest of summer fruit.

III

MATRIMONY IN HARNESS

"What eagles are we still
In matters that belong to other men;
What beetles in our own!"

The more I know of horses, the more natural I think men and women are in the unequalness of their marriages. I never yet saw a pair of horses so well matched that they pulled evenly all the time. The more skilful the driver, the less he lets the discrepancy become apparent. Going up hill, one horse generally does the greater share of work. If they pull equally up hill, sometimes they see-saw and pull in jerks on a level road. And I never saw a marriage in which both persons pulled evenly all the time, and the worst of it is, I suppose this unevenness is only what is always expected.

Having no marriage of my own to worry over, it is gratuitous when I worry over other people's. Old maids, you know, like to air their views on matrimony and bringing up children. Their theories on these subjects have this advantage—that they always hold good because they never are tried.

There never was such an unequal yoking together as the

Herricks'. Nobody has told me. This is one of the affairs which has not been confided to me. Only, I knew them both so well before they were married. I knew Bronson Herrick best, however, because I never used to see any more of Flossy than was necessary.

To begin with, I never liked her name. I have an idea that names show character. Could anybody under heaven be noble with such a name as Flossy? I believe names handicap people. I believe children are sometimes tortured by hideous and unmeaning names. But give them strong, ugly names in preference to Ina and Bessie and Flossy and such pretty-pretty names, with no meaning and no character to them. Take my own name, Ruth. If I wanted to be noble or heroic I could be; my name would not be an anomalous nightmare to attract attention to the incongruity. We cannot be too thankful to our mothers who named us Mary and Dorothy and Constance. What an inspiration to be "faithful over a few things" such a name as Constance must be!

But Flossy's mother named her—not Florence, but Flossy. I suppose she was one of those fluffy, curly, silky babies. She grew to be that kind of a girl—a Flossy girl. It speaks for itself. I suppose with that name she never had any incentive to outgrow her nature.

It came out on her wedding cards:

"Mr. and Mrs. CHARLES FAY CARLETON
request you to be present at the
marriage of their daughter
FLOSSY
to
Mr. BRONSON STURGIS HERRICK."

The contrast between the two names, hers so nonsensical and

his so dignified and strong, was no greater than that between the two people. In truth, their names were symbolic of their natures. It looked really pitiful to me.

I wondered if anybody besides Rachel English and me looked into their future with apprehension. Our misgivings, I must admit, were all for Bronson.

Ah, well-a-day! It is so easy to feel sympathy for a man you admire, especially if he is strong and loyal, and does not ask or desire it of you.

Flossy was one of those cuddling girls. She appealed to you with her eyes, and you found yourself petting her and sympathizing with her, when, if you stopped to think, you would see that she had more of everything than you had. She possessed a rich father, a beautiful house, and perfect health. Nevertheless, you found yourself asking after "poor Flossy," and your voice commiserated her if your words did not. She invariably had some trifling ill to tell you of. She had hurt her arm, or scratched her hand, or the snow made her eyes ache, or she was tired. She never seemed at liberty to enjoy herself, although she went everywhere, and seemed to do so successfully in spite of her imaginary ills, if you let her enjoy herself by telling you of them.

Everybody helped Flossy to live. Everybody protected and looked after her. There was some one on his knees continually, removing invisible brambles from her rose-leaf path. She didn't know how to do anything for herself. She never buttoned her own boots. When her maid was not with her, other people put her jacket on for her, and carried her umbrella and buttoned her gloves. Men always buttoned her gloves, and her gloves always had more buttons, and more unruly buttons, than any other gloves I ever saw. But then I am elderly.

I never knew Flossy to do anything for anybody. She never gave things away, but on Christmas and her birthdays she received remembrances from everybody. I used to make her presents without knowing why or even thinking of it. Flossy's name was on all the Christmas lists, and she used to shed tears over the kindness of her friends, and write the prettiest notes to them, so plaintive and self-deprecatory. Then they took her to drive, or did something more for her. Flossy read poetry and cried over it. She wrote poetry too, and other people cried over that.

When Bronson Herrick told me he was going to marry her, I wanted to say, "No, you are not." But I didn't. I did not even seem to be surprised, for he is so proud he would have resented any surprise on my part. He told me about it of course, knowing that I could not fail to be pleased. (His photograph is in that japanned box of mine. This smile on my face, Tabby, is rather sardonic. Why is it that men expect an old sweetheart to take an active interest in their bride-elect, and are so deadly sure that they will like each other?)

"She is the most sympathetic little thing," he said enthusias-tically. "She reminds me of you in so many ways. You are very much alike."

"Oh, thank you, Bronson Sturgis Herrick! I assure you I would cheerfully drown myself if I thought you were right about that," I exclaimed mentally.

He repeated over and over that she was "so sympathetic." He meant, of course, that she had wept over him. Flossy's tears flow like rain if you crook your finger at her, and tears wring the heart of a man like Bronson. To think he was going to marry her! I just looked at him, I remember, as he stood so straight and tall before me, and said to myself, "Well, you dear, honest, loyal, clever man! You are just the kind of a man that women fool most unmercifully. But it's nature, and you can't help it. Go and marry this Flossy girl, and commit mental suicide if you must."

"Sympathetic!"

So he married her five years ago, and became her man-servant.

When they had been married about a year, people said that Bronson was working himself to death. I, being an Old Maid, and liking to meddle with other people's business, told him that I thought he ought to take a vacation. He said he couldn't afford it. I was honestly surprised at that, because, while he was not rich, he was extremely well-to-do, with a rapidly increasing law practice. And then Flossy's father had been very generous when she married him. He was considerate enough to reply to my look.

"You know I married a rich girl. Flossy's money is her own. She has saved it—I wished her to save it, I *wished* it—and I am doing my level best to support her as nearly as possible in the way in which she has been accustomed to live. She ought to have an easier time, poor child."

So he did not take a vacation, and the summer was very hot, and when Flossy came home from Rye she found him wretchedly ill, and discovered that he had had a trained nurse for two weeks before he let her know anything about it. Then people pitied Flossy for having her summer interrupted, and Flossy felt that it was a shame; but she very willingly sat and fanned Bronson for as much as an hour every day and answered questions languidly and was pale, and people sent her flowers and were extremely sorry for her.

When Bronson became well enough to go away, as his

doctors ordered, for a complete rest, Rachel English happened to go on the same train with them, and the next day I received a letter, or rather an envelope, from her, with this single sentence enclosed: "And if she didn't make him hold her in his arms in broad daylight every step of the way, because the train jarred her back!"

(Tabby, there is no use in talking. I must stop and pull your ears. Come here and let Missis be really rough with you for a minute.)

There are some women who prefer a valet to a husband; who think that the more menial are his services in public, the more apparent is his devotion. It is a Roman-chariot-wheel idea, which degrades both the man and the woman in the eyes of the spectators. I wrote to Rachel, and said in the letter, "One horse in the span always does most of the pulling, you know, especially uphill." And Rachel wrote back, "Wouldn't I just like to drive this pair, though!"

Bronson had his ideals before he was married, as most men have, concerning the kind of a home he hoped for. He always said that it was not so much what your home was, as how it was. He believed that a home consisted more in the feelings and aims of its inmates than in rugs and jardinieres. He said to me once, "The oneness of two people could make a home in Sahara."

He was ambitious, too, feeling within himself that power which makes orators and statesmen, but needing the approval and encouragement of some one who also realized his capabilities, to enable him to do his best. He himself was the one who was sympathetic, if he had only known it. His nature responded with the utmost readiness to whatever appealed to him from the side of right or justice.

He had noble hopes in many directions, hopes which inspired me to believe in his truth and goodness, aside from his capabilities for achieving greatness. His eagle sight, which read through other men's shams and pretences; his moral sense, which bade him shun even the appearance of evil, not only permitted, but urged him, seemingly, into this marriage with Flossy, by which he effectually cut himself off from his dearest aspirations. One by one I have seen him relinquish them, holding to them lovingly to the last. The hours at home, which he intended to give to study and research, have been sacrificed to the petting and nursing of a perfectly well woman, who demanded it of him. His home life, where he had dreamed of a congenial atmosphere, where the centripetal force should be the love of wife and children, merged into frequent journeys for Flossy—who would have been happy if she never had been obliged to stay in one place over a week—and a shifting of their one child Rachel into the care of nurses, because Flossy fretted at the care of her and demanded all of Bronson's time for herself.

Thus was Bronson's life being twisted and bent from its natural course. Was it a weakness in him? To be sure he might have shown his strength by breaking loose from family ties, and, hardening his heart to his wife's plaints, have carried out his ambitions with some degree of success. He did attempt this, nor did he fail in his career. He was called a fairly successful man. I dare say the majority of people never knew that he was created for grander things. But something was sapping his energy at the fountain-head. Was he realizing that he had helped to shatter his ideals with his own hand?

I never am so well satisfied with my lot of single-blessedness as when I contemplate the sort of wife Flossy makes. That may sound arrogant, but this is a secret session of human nature, when arrogance and all native-born sins are permissible.

Flossy is perfectly unconscious of the spectacle she presents to the world. Ah, me! I know it is said, "Judge not, that ye be not judged." I might have made him just such a wife, I suppose. O heavens! no, I shouldn't. Tabby, that is making humility go a little too far.

IV

WOMEN AS LOVERS

"In every clime and country
There lives a Man of Pain,
Whose nerves, like chords of lightning,
Bring fire into his brain:
To him a whisper is a wound,
A look or sneer, a blow;
More pangs he feels in years or months
Than dunce-throng'd ages know."

I have had such a curious experience. I have been confided in, twice in one day. Two more bits out of other lives have been given to me, and it is astonishing to see how well they piece into mine.

To begin with, Rachel English came in early. There is something particularly auspicious about Rachel. She fits me like a glove. She never jars nor grates. When she is here, I am comfortable; when she is gone, I miss something. If I see a fine painting, or hear magnificent music, I think of Rachel before any other thought comes into my mind. One involuntarily associates her with anything wonderfully fine in art or literature, with the perfect assurance that she will be sympathetic and appreciative. She understands the deep, inarticulate emotions in the kindred way you have a right to expect of your lover, and which you are oftenest disappointed in, if you do expect it of him. If I were a man, I should be in love with Rachel.

Her sensitiveness through every available channel makes her of no use to general society. Blundering people tread on her; malicious ones tear her to pieces. Rachel ought to be caged, and only approached by clever people who have brains enough to appreciate her. I should like to be her keeper. But her organization is too closely allied to that of genius to be happy, unless with certain environments which it is too good to believe will ever surround her. She is so clever that she is perfectly helpless. If you knew her, this would not be a paradox. Possibly it isn't anyway.

I do not say that Rachel is perfect. She would be desperately uncomfortable as a friend if she were. Her failings are those belonging to a frank, impulsive, generous nature, which I myself find it easy to forgive. Her gravest fault is a witty tongue. That which many people would give years of their lives to possess is what she has shed the most tears over and which she most liberally detests in herself. She calls it her private demon, and says she knows that one of the devils, in the woman who was possessed of seven, was the devil of wit.

Wit is a weapon of defence, and was no more intended to be an attribute of woman than is a knowledge of fire-arms or a fondness for mice. A witty woman is an anomaly, fit only for literary circles and to be admired at a distance.

It is of no use to advise Rachel to curb her tongue. So tender-hearted that the sight of an animal in pain makes her faint; so humble-minded that she cannot bear to receive an apology,

Lilian Bell

but, no matter what has been the offence, cuts it off short and hastens to accept it before it is uttered, with the generous assurance that she, too, has been to blame; yet she wounds cruelly, but unconsciously, with her tongue, which cleaves like a knife, and holds up your dearest, most private foibles on stilettos of wit for the public to mock at. Not that she is personal in her allusions, but her thorough knowledge of the philosophy of human nature and the deep, secret springs of human action lead her to witty, satirical generalizations, which are so painfully true that each one of her hearers goes home hugging a personal affront, while poor Rachel never dreams of lacerated feelings until she meets averted faces or hears a whisper of her heinous sin. This grieves her wofully, but leaves her with no mode of redress, for who dare offer balm to wounded vanity? I believe her when she says she "never wilfully planted a thorn in any human breast."

She scarcely had entered before I saw that she had something on her mind. And it was not long before she began to confide, but in an impersonal way.

There is something which makes you hold your breath before you enter the inner nature of some one who has extraordinary depth. You feel as if you were going to find something different and interesting, and possibly difficult or explosive. It is dark, too, yet you feel impelled to enter. It is like going into a cave.

Most people are afraid of Rachel. Sometimes I am. But it is the alluring, hysterical fear which makes a child say, "Scare me again."

Imagine such a girl in love. Rachel is in love. She would not say with whom—naturally. At least, naturally for Rachel. I felt rather helpless, but as I knew that all she wanted was an intelligent sympathizer, not verbal assistance, I was willing to blunder a little. I knew she would speedily set me right.

"You are too clever to marry," I said at a hazard.

"That is one of the most popular of fallacies," she answered me crushingly. "Why can't clever women marry, and make just as good wives as the others? Why can't a woman bend her cleverness to see that her house is in order, and her dinners well cooked, and buttons sewed on, as well as to discuss new books and keep pace with her husband intellectually? Do you suppose because I know Greek that I cannot be in love? Do you suppose because I went through higher mathematics that I never pressed a flower he gave me? Do you imagine that Biology kills blushing in a woman? Do you think that Philosophy keeps me from crying myself to sleep when I think he doesn't care for me, or growing idiotically glad when he tells me he does? What rubbish people write upon this subject! Even Pope proved that he was only a man when he said,

> "'Love seldom haunts the breast where learning lies,
> And Venus sets ere Mercury can rise.'

"Did you ever read such foolishness?"

"Often, my dear, often. But console yourself. A wiser than Pope says, 'The learned eye is still the loving one.'"

"Browning, of course. I ought not to be surprised that the prince of poets should be clever enough to know that. It is from his own experience. 'Who writes to himself, writes to an eternal public.' You see, Ruth, men can't help looking at the question from the other side, because they form the other side. You might cram a woman's head with all the wisdom of the ages, and while it would frighten every man who came near her into hysterics, it wouldn't keep her from going down

Lilian Bell

abjectly before some man who had sense enough to know that higher education does not rob a woman of her womanliness. Depend upon it, Ruth, when it does, she would have been unwomanly and masculine if she hadn't been able to read. And it is the man who marries a woman of brains who is going to get the most out of this life."

"Men don't want clever wives," I said feebly.

"Clever men don't. Why is it that all the brightest men we know have selected girls who looked pretty and have coddled them? Look at Bronson and Flossy. That man is lonesome, I tell you, Ruth. He actually hungers and thirsts for his intellectual and moral affinity, and yet even he did not have the sense—the astuteness—to select a wife who would have stood at his side, instead of one who lay in a wad at his feet. Oh, the bungling marriages that we see! I believe one reason is that like seldom marries like. For my part I do not believe in the marriage of opposites. Look at Robert Browning and his wife. That is my ideal marriage. Their art and brains were married, as well as their hands and hearts. It is pure music to think of it. And, to me, the most pathetic poem in the English language is Browning's 'Andrea del Sarto.'"

"Isn't it strange to see the kind of men who love clever women like you? You never could have brought yourself to marry any of them, expecting to find them congenial. They would have admired you in dumb silence, until they grew tired of feeling your superiority; after that—what?"

"The deluge, I suppose. Ruth, I don't see how a woman with any self-respect can marry until she meets her master. That is high treason, isn't it? But it is one of those sentient bits of truth which we never mention in society. The man I marry must have a stronger will and a greater brain than I have, or I should rule him. I'll never marry until I find a man who knows more than I do. Yet, as to these other men who have loved me—you know what a tender place a woman has in her heart for the men who have wanted to marry her. My intellect repudiated, but my heart cherishes them still. Odd things, hearts. Sometimes I wish we didn't have any when they ache so. I feel like disagreeing with all the poets to-day, because they will not say what I believe. Do you remember this, from Beaumont and Fletcher,

"'Of all the paths that lead to woman's love
Pity's the straightest'?

"Men are fond of saying that, I notice, but I don't think we women bear out the truth. I couldn't love a man I pitied. I could love one I was proud of, or afraid of, but one I pitied? Never. It is more true to say it of men. I believe plenty of girls obtain husbands by virtue of their weakness, their loneliness, their helplessness, their—anything which makes a man pity them. Pleasant thought, isn't it, for a woman who loves her own sex and wishes it held its head up better! You may say that it is this sort who receive more of the attentions that women love, chivalry and tenderness and devotion. But if all or any of these were inspired by pity, I'd rather not have them. I would rather a man would be rough and brusque with me, if he loved me heroically, than to see him fling his coat in the mud for me to step on, because he pitied my weakness. Do you know, Ruth, I think men are a good deal more human than women. You can work them out by algebra (for they never have more than one unknown quantity, and in the woman problem there would be more x's than anything else), and you can go by rules and get the answer. But nothing ever calculated or evolved can get the final answer to one woman—though they do say she is fond of the last word! We understand ourselves intuitively, and we understand men by study, yet we are made the receivers, not the givers; the chosen, not the choosers. It really is an absurd dispensation when you view it apart from sentiment, yet I, for one, would not have it changed. I should not mind being Cupid for a while, though, and giving him a few ideas in the mating line.

"I think women are often misjudged. Men seem to think that all we want is to be loved. Now, it isn't all that I want. If I had to choose between being loved by a man—*the* man, let us say—and not loving him at all, or loving him very dearly and not being loved by him, I would choose the latter, for I think that more happiness comes from loving than from being loved."

"Why *don't* you marry somebody?" I asked in an agony of entreaty, for fear all of this would be wasted on me, an Old Maid, rather than upon some man. She shook her head.

"It needs a compelling, not a persuasive, power to win a woman. No man who takes me like this," closing her thumb and forefinger as if holding a butterfly, "can have me. The one who dares to take me like this," clenching her hand, "will get me. But he will not come."

Then I walked with her to the door, and she bent over me, and whispered something about my being a "blessed comfort" to her, and went away. Ah, Tabby, my dear, it is worth while being an Old Maid to be a blessed comfort to anybody. But I would just like to ask you, as a cat of intelligence, what in the world I did for her!

Imagine some man making that girl care for him so much. For, of course, it is somebody. A girl does not say such things about the abstract man.

I was in an uplifted state of mind all day, as I am always after a talk with Rachel, and when Percival came in the evening, I felt that I could deluge him with my gathered sentiment, and he would be receptive. Besides, Percival has a positive genius for understanding. I did not know it, however, this morning. I seldom know as much in the morning as I do at night.

Percival approves of sentiment. He said once that a life which had principle and sentiment needed little else, for principle was to stand upon, and sentiment was to beautify with. He said this after I had told him rather apologetically that I wished there was more sentiment in the world, because I liked it. Is it strange that I like Percival? You can't help admiring people who approve of you.

Percival is a genius. People in general do not recognize this fact. He is an inarticulate genius. Men feel that he is in some occult way different from them, yet they do not know just how. Nor will they ever take the trouble to study out a problem in human nature, either in man or woman, unless they are philosophers.

Women care for Percival in proportion to their intuitions. You must comprehend him synthetically. You cannot dissect him. With generous appreciation and sympathetic encourage-ment, Percival's genius would become articulate. To discover it he must needs marry—but he must wait for the hundredth woman. This, of course, he will not do. If he can find a Flossy, he will go down on his knees to her, when she ought to be on hers to him; metaphorical knees, in this case.

I am very much afraid he has found her. He is in love. You can always tell when a man is in love, Tabby, especially if he is not the lovering kind and has never been troubled in that way before. The best kind of love has to be so intuitive that it often is grandly, heroically awkward. Depend upon it, Tabby, a man who is dainty and pretty and unspeakably smooth when he makes love to you, has had altogether too much practice.

Percival knows that he is in love—that is one great step in the right direction. But he is in that first partly alarmed, partly curious frame of mind that a man would be in who touched his broken arm for the first time to see how much it hurt. Whoever she is, he loves her deeply and thinks she never can care for him. He did not tell me this. If he thought that I knew it, he would wonder how in the world I found it out. Women are born lovers. They have to do the bulk of the loving all through the world. I told Percival so. At first he seemed surprised; then he said that it was true. I believe some men could go through life without loving anybody on earth. But the woman never lived who could do it. A woman must love something—even if she hasn't anything better to love than a pug-dog or herself.

"Why aren't women the choosers?" said Percival seriously. The same question twice in one day, Tabby. "Whenever I think of understanding the question of love, I wish for a woman's intuitions. Women know so much about it. They absorb the whole question at a glance. But, with so many different kinds of women, how is a man to know anything?"

I always liked Percival, but a woman never likes a man so well as when he acknowledges his helplessness in her particular line of knowledge, and throws himself on her mercy. Mentally, I at once began to feel motherly towards Percival, and clucked around him like an old hen. He went on to say that men often are not so blind that they cannot see the prejudices and complexities of a woman's nature, but they are not constituted to understand them by intuition as women understand men. "The masculine mind," he said, "is but ill-attuned to the subtle harmonies of the feminine heart."

I was secretly very much pleased at this remark, but I made myself answer as became an Old Maid, just to make him continue without self-consciousness. If I had blushed and thanked him, he would have gone home.

"They set these things down to the natural curiousness and contrariness of women, and often despise what they cannot comprehend."

He answered me with the heightened consciousness and slight irritation of a man who has been in that fault, but has seen and mended it.

"All men do not. Still, how can they help it at times?"

Then, Tabby, I went a-sailing. I launched out on my favorite theme.

"Men must needs study women. Often the terror with which some men regard these—to us—perfectly transparent complexities, could be avoided if they would analyze the cause with but half the patience they display in the case of an ailing trotter. But no; either they edge carefully away from such dangers as they previously have experienced, or, if they blunder into new ones, they give the woman a sealskin and trust to time to heal the breach."

I thought of the Asburys when I said that. But Percival ruminated upon it, as if it touched his own case. A very good thing about Percival is that he does not think he knows everything. It encourages me to believe in his genius. To rouse him from a brown-study over this Flossy girl, I said rather recklessly,

"I should like to be a man for a while, in order to make love to two or three women. I would do it in a way which should

Lilian Bell

not shock them with its coarseness or starve them with its poverty. As it is now, most women deny themselves the expression of the best part of their love, because they know it will be either a puzzle or a terror to their lovers."

Percival was vitally interested at once.

"Is that really so?" he asked. "Do you suppose any of them withhold anything from such a fear?" His face was so uplifted that I plunged on, thoroughly in the dark, but, like Barkis, "willin'." If I could be of use to him in an emergency, I was only too happy.

"Men never realize the height of the pedestal where women in love place them, nor do they know with how many perfections they are invested nor how religiously women keep themselves deceived on the subject. They cannot comprehend the succession of little shocks which is caused by the real man coming in contact with the ideal. And if they did understand, they would think that such mere trifles should not affect the genuine article of love, and that women simply should overlook foibles, and go on loving the damaged article just as blindly as before. But what man could view his favorite marble tumbling from its pedestal continually, and losing first a finger, then an arm, then a nose, and would go on setting it up each time, admiring and reverencing in the mutilated remains the perfect creation which first enraptured him? He wouldn't take the trouble to fill up the nicks and glue on the lost fingers as women do to their idols. He wouldn't even try to love it as he used to do. When it began to look too battered up, he would say, 'Here, put this thing in the cellar and let's get it out of the way.'"

Percival listened with specific interest, and admitted its truth with a fair-mindedness surprising even in him.

"Do you suppose it is possible for a man ever to thoroughly understand a woman?" he asked, with a retrospective slowness, directed, I was sure, towards that empty-headed sweetheart of his.

"I really do not know," I said honestly. "I think if he tried with all his might he could."

"Do you think—you know me better than any one else does—do you think *I* could, if I gave my whole mind to it?"

"You, if anybody." I answered him with the occasional absolute truthfulness which occurs between a man and a woman when they are completely lifted out of themselves. Something more than mere pleasure shone in his eyes. It was as if I had reached his soul.

"If no man ever has been all that a woman in love really believes him, the best a man could do would be to take care that she never found out her mistake," he said slowly.

"Exactly," I said; "you are getting on. It is only another way of making yourself live up to her ideal of you."

"Supposing after all, that the woman I love will have none of me," he said, unconsciously slipping from the third person to the first.

"I wouldn't admit even the possibility if I were a man. I would besiege the fortress. I would sit on her front doorstep until she gave in. Don't ask her to have you. Tell her you are going to have her whether or no," I cried, thinking of Rachel's words. He looked so encouraged that I am afraid I have sent him post-haste to the Flossy girl, and gotten him into life-long trouble. But I had gone too far. I quite hurried, in my accidental endeavor to shipwreck him.

"Men do not understand these things, because they will not give time enough to them. Real love-making requires the patience, the tenderness, the sympathy which women alone possess in the highest degree. Possibly she loves you deeply, only you do not believe it. Gauged by a woman's love, many men love, marry, and die, without even approximating the real grand passion themselves, or comprehending that which they have inspired, for no one but a woman can fathom a woman's love."

I couldn't help going on after I started, for he was thinking of the other woman, and looking at me in a way that would have made my heart turn over, if I hadn't been an Old Maid, and known that his look was not for me.

Then he ground my rings into my hand until I nearly shrieked with the pain, and said, "God bless you!" very hoarsely, and dashed out of the house before I could pull myself together. *I* say so too. God bless me, what have I done? I've sent him straight to that Flossy girl. I feel it. I've smoothed out something between them. I have accidentally made him articulate, and articulation in such a man as Percival is overpowering. He is a murdered man, and mine is the hand that slew him.

Tabby, old maids are a public nuisance, not to say dangerous. They ought to be suppressed.

*   *   *   *   *

I wonder if he will burst in upon her with that look upon his face!

V

THE HEART OF A COQUETTE

"Strange, that a film of smoke can blot a star!"

He did. And the woman was—Rachel. Tabby, I never was better pleased with myself in my life. I love old maids. I think that whenever they are accidental they are perfectly lovely. But *what* a risk I ran!

I did not know a thing about it until I received their wedding-cards. It was just like Rachel not to tell me, and it was insufferably stupid in me not to use the few wits I am possessed of, and see how matters stood. But my fears and tremors were that Frankie Taliaferro would get him, so I have watched her all this time. Percival laughed almost scornfully when I told him this, and said I had been barking up the wrong tree. I retaliated by saying that if they had been ordinary lovers, I never could have made such a mistake, and they took it as a great compliment. When I consider the general run of engaged people, I am inclined to agree with them. Everybody seems to think they are making an experiment of marriage, because they are so much alike. But, then, doesn't every one who marries at all, Jew or Gentile, black or white, bond or free, make an experiment? I myself have no fear as to how the Percival experiment will turn out. Rachel says that they are so similar in all their tastes and ideals that if she were a man she would be Percival, and if he were a woman he would be Rachel. "Then you still would have a chance to marry each other," I said frivolously. But she assented with a depth of feeling which ignored my feeble attempt to be cheerful. "Yet," she continued, "there is a subtle, alluring difference in our thoughts; just enough to add piquancy, not irritation, to a discussion. I do not love white, and he does not love black, as so many husbands and wives do. We both love gray; different tones of gray, but still gray. It is very restful." The Percivals are not only restful to themselves, but to others. They used to be in the highly irritable, nervous state of those whose sensitive organisms are a little too fine for this world. I never objected to it myself, but I have said before that Rachel was of no use to ordinary society, and Percival was little better. When people failed to understand her, she retired into herself with a dignity which was mistaken for ill-temper. She is too refined and high-minded to defend herself against the "slings and arrows of outrageous" people, although if she would, she could exterminate them with her wit. And some could so easily be spared. It seems, too, that she is great enough to be a target, so she is under fire continually. This, while it causes her exquisite suffering, is from no fault of her own—save the unforgivable one of being original. "A frog spat at a glow-worm. 'Why do you spit at me?' said the glow-worm. 'Why do you shine so?' said the frog." And as to Percival—the man I used to know was Percival in embryo. He is maturing now, and is radiant in Rachel's sympathetic comprehension of him. He refers to the time before he knew her as his "protoplasmic state," as indeed it was. But there are a good many of us who would be willing to remain protoplasm all our lives to possess a tithe of his genius—you and I among the number, Tabby. You needn't look at me so reproachfully out of your old-gold eyes. You know you would.

You have seen Sallie Cox, haven't you? Then you know how it jarred my nerves to have her rush in upon me when my mind was full of the Percivals.

Sallie has flirted joyously through life thus far, and has appeared to have about as little heart as any girl I ever knew. Sallie is the *sauce piquante* in one's life—absolutely necessary at times to make things taste at all, but a little of her goes a long way. At least so I thought until to-day.

"I've got something to tell you, Ruth," she said, "so come with me, and we will take a little drive before going to cooking-school."

I went, knowing, of course, that she wanted to confide something about some of her lovers.

"I am going to be married," she announced coldly. "It's Payson Osborne this time, and I'm really going to see the thing through. It's rather a joke on me, because it commenced this way. I was sick of lovers, and some of the last had been so unpleasant, not to say rude, when I threw them over, that I thought I would take a vacation. So when I met Payson, I said, 'What do you say to a Platonic friendship?' It sounds harmless, you know, Ruth, and he, not knowing me at all, assented. If he had been a man who knew of my checkered career, he would have refused, suspecting, of course, that I was going to flirt with him under a new name. But, as I was serious this time, I knew it was all right. So we began. I suppose you know he is enormously rich, besides being so handsome, and there will not be a girl in town who won't say I raised heaven and earth to get him; but I don't mind telling you, Ruth—because you are such an old dear, and never are bothered with lovers(!); besides, it will do me good to tell it, and I know you will never betray me— that I never cared for any man on earth except Winston

Percival. You needn't jump, and look as though the house was on fire. It's the solemn truth, and I never dreamed that he cared for Rachel until he married her. Mind you, he never pretended to love me. It is every bit one-sided, and I don't care if it is. I am glad that a frivolous, shallow-minded, rattle-brained thing like me had sense enough to fall in love with the most glorious man that ever came into her life. I shouldn't have made him half as good a wife as Rachel does—I really feel as if they were made for each other—but he would have made a woman of me. I'm honestly glad he is so happy, and things are much more suitable as they are, for Payson is a thorough-going society man, and doesn't ask much in a wife or he wouldn't have me, and he doesn't expect much from a wife or he couldn't get me.

"Perhaps you don't know that a girl who makes a business of wearing scalps at her belt never stands a bit of a chance with a man she really loves, for she is afraid to practise on him the wiles which she knows from experience have been success- ful with scores of others, because she feels that he will see through them, and scorn her as she scorns herself in his presence. She loses her courage, she loses control of herself, and, being used to depend on 'business,' as actors say, to carry out her role successfully, she finds that she is only reading her lines, and reading them very badly too. If you could have seen me with Percival, you would know what I mean. I was dull, uninteresting, poky—no more the Sallie Cox that other men know than I am you. He absorbed my personality. I didn't care for myself or how I appeared. I only wanted him to shine and be his natural, brilliant self. I never could have helped him in his work. The most I could have hoped to do would have been not to hinder him. I would have been the gainer—it would have been the act of a home missionary for him to marry me."

She laughed drearily.

"Isn't it horribly immoral in me to sit here and talk in this way about a married man? It's a wonder it doesn't turn the color of the cushions. If you hear of my having the brougham relined, Ruth, you will know why. Ruth, I am so miserable at times it seems to me that I shall die. I'd love to cry this minute—cry just as hard as I could, and scream, and beat my head against something hard—how do you do, Mrs. Asbury?—but instead, I have to bow from the windows to people, and remember that I am supposed to be the complaisant bride-elect of the catch of the season. It is a judgment on me, Ruth, to find that I have a heart, when I have always gone on the principle that nobody had any. Yes—how-de-do, Miss Culpepper? excuse me a minute, Ruth, while I hate that girl. What has she done to me? Oh, nothing to speak of—she only had the bad taste to fall in love with the man I am going to marry. Writes him notes all the time, making love to him, which he promptly shows to me—oh, we are not very honorable, or very upright, or very anything good in the Osborne matrimonial arrangement. Anybody but you would hate me for all this I've told you, but I know you are pitying me with all your soul, because you know the empty-headed Sallie Cox carries with her a very sore heart, and that it will take more than Payson Osborne has got to give to heal it. I call him Pay sometimes, but he hates it. I only do it when I think how much he does pay for a very bad bargain. But he doesn't care, so why should I?

"It really does seem odd, when I look back on it, to see how easy it was to get him, when all the time I was perfectly indifferent to him, and received his attentions on the Platonic basis to keep him from making love to me. I really think I never had any one to care for me in so exactly the way I like, and to be so easy in his demands, and to think me so altogether perfect and charming, no matter what I do. It was because I was absolutely indifferent to him. I never cared when he came. I never cared when he went. Other lovers fussed and quarrelled and were jealous and disagreeable when I flirted with other men, but Payson never cared. He didn't tease me, you know. And whenever he said anything, I could look innocent and say, 'Is that Platonic friendship?' So he would have to subside. I know he thought some of my indifference was assumed, for when he told me about Miss Culpepper he thought I would be vexed. I *was* vexed, but I had presence of mind not to show it. I only laughed and made no comment at all—asked him what time it was, I believe. Then when he looked so disappointed and sulky, I knew I was right, and I patted Sallie Cox on the head for being so clever—so clever as not to care, chiefly. There is nothing, absolutely nothing, you cannot do with a man who loves you, if you don't care a speck for him. And the luxury of perfect indifference! Emotions are awfully wearing, Ruth. I wonder that these emotional women like Rachel get on at all. I should think they would die of the strain. Men are always deadly afraid of such women. I believe Payson wouldn't stop running till he got to California if I should burst into tears and not be able to tell him instantly just exactly where my neuralgia had jumped to. No unknown waverings and quaverings of the heart for my good Osborne. There goes Alice Asbury again. I am dying to tell you something. You know why she hates me, and understand why she treats me so abominably? Well, Asbury gave her the same engagement ring he gave me, and she doesn't know it. Rich, isn't it? Here we are at the cooking-school. I am so glad I can slam a carriage-door without being rude. It is such a relief to one's overcharged feelings."

Tabby, dear, if your head ever spun round and round at some of the confidences I have bestowed upon you, I can sympathize with you, for, as I went into that class, my feelings were so wrenched and twisted that I was as limp as cooked macaroni. You will excuse the simile, but that was one of the articles at cooking-school to-day, and when the teacher took it up on a fork, it did express my state of mind so exquisitely that I cannot forbear to use it.

Sallie Cox! Well, I am amazed. Who would think that that bright, saucy, clever little flirt, who rides on the crest of the wave always, could have such a heart history? And Percival of all men! I wonder what he would say if he knew. I don't know what to think about her marrying Payson Osborne. The last thing she whispered to me as we came out of cooking-school was, "Don't be too sorry for me because I am going to marry him. Believe me, it is the very best thing that could happen to me."

I am very fond of the girl to-night. What a pity it is that everybody does not know her as she really is! No one understands her, and she has flirted so outrageously with most of the men that the girls' friendship for her is very hollow. A few, of whom Alice Asbury is one, dare to show this quite plainly, and of course Sallie doesn't like it. She pretends not to care for women's friendship, but she does. She would love to be friendly with all the girls, but they remember the misery she has made them suffer, and won't have it.

Still, there is no doubt that she is marrying the man most of them want, so that again she triumphs. But, unless I am much mistaken, even as Mrs. Payson Osborne it will take her a long time to recover her place with the women which she has lost by having so many of their sweethearts and brothers in love with her.

Ah, Tabby, what a deal of secret misery there is in the world! Everybody will envy Sallie Cox and think that she is the luckiest girl, and Sallie will smile and pretend—for what other course is left to her, and who can blame women who pretend under such circumstances? Perhaps there are reasons

Lilian Bell

just as good for many other pretenders in this world. Who knows? We would be gentler if we knew more.

There will be other sore hearts besides Sallie's at her wedding. I had heard before that Miss Culpepper was quite desperate over Osborne, but, as she was a girl whom everybody thought a lady, I had no idea that she had gone so far as Sallie says. Osborne probably didn't object to being made love to. A man of his stamp would not be over-refined. Strange, now, Sallie does not love Osborne herself, but she promptly hates every other girl who dares to do it. Aren't girls queer?

Then there are a score of men who will gnash their teeth for Sallie—so many men love these Sallie Coxes.

Frankie Taliaferro, the Kentucky beauty, who is staying with her this winter, tells me that Sallie has had several dreadful scenes with discarded suitors—that one said he would forbid the banns, and another threatened to shoot himself if she really married Osborne.

I wonder how many marriages there really are where both are perfectly free to marry. I mean, no secret entanglements on either side, no other man wanting the bride, no girl bitterly jealous of her. I never heard of one—not among the people *I* know, at least.

Oh, Tabby, think of all the fusses people keep out of who promptly settle down at the appointed time and become peaceful old maids. How sensible we were, Tabby, you and Missis.

But doesn't it seem to you that people marry from very mixed motives? I used to have an idea—when I was painfully young, of course—that they married because they were so fortunate as to fall in love with each other. Are you quite sure that foolish notion is out of your head too?

Lilian Bell

VI

THE LONELY CHILDHOOD OF A CLEVER CHILD

"Is it so bad, then, to be misunderstood?... To be great is to be   misunderstood."

I have been away since early last summer, and consequently never had seen Flossy's new baby until the newness had worn off, and it had arrived at the dignity of a backbone, and had left its wobbly period far behind. I am in mortal terror of a very little baby. It feels so much like a sponge, yet lacks the sponge's recuperative qualities. I am always afraid if I dent it the dents will stay in. You know they don't in a sponge.

As soon as I came home, of course I went to see Flossy's baby, and was very much disconcerted to discover that she had named it for me. I was afraid, I remember, that she would want to name the first girl for me, but she did not. She named her after Rachel. I had an uncomfortable idea, however, that my name had been discussed and vetoed, by either Flossy or Bronson. But this time the baby is named Ruth, and I found that it was all Flossy's doing.

I was irritated without knowing why. I didn't want anybody to know it though, and so I was vexed when Bronson said to me, "I couldn't help it, Ruth." There was no use in pretending not to understand. I could with some men, but not with Bronson. He is too magnificently honest himself, and uplifts me by expecting me to be equally so. Nevertheless I failed him in one particular, for I answered him in my loftiest manner, "I am not at all displeased. It is a great compliment, I am sure."

There is nothing so uncivil at times as to be cuttingly polite. What I said wasn't so at all. But a woman is obliged to defend herself from a man who reads her like an open book.

Flossy does not like children, and poor little Rachel never has had a life of roses. Flossy says children are such a care and require so much attention.

"Rachel was all that I could attend to, and here all winter I have had another one on my hands to keep me at home, and make me lose sleep, and grow old before my time. I don't see why such burdens have to be put upon people. Children are too thick in this world any way."

She fretted on in this strain for some time, until Bronson looked up and said,

"Don't, Flossy. You don't mean what you say. Do tell her the little thing is welcome."

"I do mean what I say," answered Flossy.

Then, as Bronson left the room abruptly, Flossy said,

"And I was determined to name her after you. Bronson didn't want me to. He said you wouldn't thank me for it, but I told him that Rachel Percival was quite delighted with her namesake."

I hid my indignantly smarting eyes in the folds of the baby's dress, as I held her up before my face, and made her laugh at the flowers in my hat. Flossy thought I was not listening to her with sufficient interest; so she got up and crossed the room with that little stumble of hers, which used to be so taking with the men when she was a girl, and took Ruth away from me.

There was a great contrast between the two children. Rachel Herrick is a shy child, with a delicate, refined face, lighted by wonderful gray eyes like Bronson's. I do not understand her. She seems afraid of me, and I confess I am equally afraid of her. Even Rachel Percival does not get on with her very well, although she has bravely tried. The child spends most of her time in the library, devouring all the books she can lay her hands on. Little Ruth is a round, soft, fluffy baby, all dimples and smiles and good-nature, willing to roll or crawl into anybody's lap or affections. A very good baby to exhibit, for strangers delight in her, and pet her just as people always have petted Flossy. Rachel stands mutely watching all such demonstrations, her pale face rigid with some emotion, and her eyes brilliant and hard. She is not a child one would dare take liberties with. No one ever pets her. Flossy complains continually of her to visitors and to Bronson, so that Bronson has gotten into the way of reproving her mechanically whenever his eye rests upon her. Her very presence, always silent, always inwardly critical, seems to irritate her parents. She was not doing a thing, but sitting sedately, with a heavy book on her lap, watching the baby, with that curious expression on her face; but Flossy couldn't let her alone.

"Baby loves her mother, doesn't she? She is not like naughty sister Rachel, who won't do anything but read, and never loves anybody but herself. Sister says bad things to poor sick mamma, and mamma can't love her, can she? But mamma loves her pretty, sweet baby, so she does."

Rachel glanced at me with a hunted look in her eyes which wrung my heart. But, before I could think, she slid down and the big book fell with a crash to the floor. She ran towards the baby with a wicked look on her small face, and the baby leaped and held out its hands, but Rachel clenched her teeth, and slapped the outstretched hand as she rushed past her and out of the room.

Poor little Ruth looked at the red place on her hand a minute, then her lip quivered, and she began to cry pitifully.

I instinctively looked to see Flossy gather her up to comfort her. It is so easy to dry a child's tears with a little love. But she rang for the nurse and fretfully exclaimed,

"Isn't that just like her! I declare I can't see why a child of mine should have such a wicked temper. Here, Simpson, take this young nuisance and stop her crying. Oh, poor little me! Ruth, I'm thankful that you have no children to wear your life out."

I dryly remarked that I too considered it rather a cause for gratitude, and came away.

Poor little Rachel Herrick! Unlovely as her action was, I cannot help thinking that it was unpremeditated; that it was the unexpected result of some strong inward feeling. She looked like one who was justly indignant, and, considering what Flossy had said, I felt that her anger was righteous. That her disposition is unfortunate cannot be denied. She seems already to be an Ishmaelite, for whenever she speaks it

Lilian Bell

is to fling out a remark so biting in its sarcasm, so bitter and satirical, that Flossy is afraid of her, and Bronson reproves her with unnecessary severity, because her offence is that of a grown person, which her childish stature mocks. Other children both fear and hate her. They resent her cleverness. They like to use her wits to organize their plays, but they never include her, for she always wants to lead, feeling, doubtless, that she inherently possesses the qualities of a leader, and chafing, as a heroic soul must, under inferior management. Flossy makes her go out to play regularly with them every day, but it is a pitiful sight, for she feels her unpopularity, and children are cruel to each other with the cruelty of vindictive dulness; so Rachel, after standing about among them forlornly for a while, like a stray robin among a flock of little owls, comes creeping in alone, and sits down in the library with a book. She is the loneliest child I ever knew. If she cared, people would at least be sorry for her; but she seems to love no one, never seeks sympathy if she is hurt, repels all attempts to ease pain, and cures herself with her beloved books. I never saw any one kiss or offer to pet her, but they make a great fuss over the baby, and Rachel watches them with glittering eyes. I thought once that it was jealousy, and, going up to her, laid my hand on her head, but she shook it off as if it had been a viper, and ran out of the room.

I had grown very fond of my namesake, and used to go there when Flossy was away, and sit in the nursery. The nurse told me once that Mrs. Herrick saw so little of the baby that it was afraid, and cried at the sight of her. I reproved her for speaking in that manner of her mistress, but she only tossed her head knowingly, and I dropped the subject. Servants often are aware of more than we give them credit for.

Saturday before Easter I stopped at Flossy's, but she was not at home. I left some flowers for her, and asked to see the baby, but the nurse said she was asleep.

Easter morning I did not go to church, and Rachel Percival came early in the afternoon to see if I were ill. While she was here this note arrived by a messenger:

> "DEAR RUTH,—I know you will grieve for me when I tell you that our baby went away from us quite suddenly this morning, while the Easter bells were ringing so joyfully. They rang the knell of a mother's heart, for they rang my baby's spirit into Paradise.
>
> "I feel, through my tears, that it is better so, for she will bind me closer to Heaven when I think that she, in her purity, awaits me there.
>
> "Hoping to see you very soon, I am
> "Your loving
> FLOSSY.
>
> "P.S.—Bronson seems to feel the baby's death to a truly astonishing degree.
>
> F. H."

I flung the note across to Rachel, and, putting my head down on my two arms, I cried just as hard as I could cry.

Rachel read it, then tore it into twenty bits, and ground her heel into the fragments.

"Why, Rachel Percival! what is the matter?"

"She wasn't even at home. She was at church. She must have been. She told me that Bronson was afraid to have her leave the baby, and wouldn't come himself, but that she didn't think anything was the matter with it, and wouldn't be tied down. Then such a note so soon afterwards! Ruth, what is that woman made of?"

We went together to Flossy's. She came across the room to meet us, supported by Bronson. She stumbled two or three times in the attempt. Tears were running down Bronson's face, and he wiped them away quite humbly, as if he did not mind our seeing them in the least. I could not bear to watch him, so I slipped out of the room and went upstairs.

"In here, 'm," said the nurse; "and Miss Rachel is here too. She won't move that far from the cradle, and she hasn't shed a tear."

Ruth lay peacefully in her little lace crib, covered with violets, and beside her, rigid and white and tearless, stood Rachel. I was almost afraid of the child as I looked at her. She turned her great eyes upon me dumbly, with so exactly Bronson's expression in them that all at once I understood her. I knelt down beside her, and gathering her little tense frame all up in my arms, I began whispering to her. The tears rolled down her cheeks, and soon she was crying hysterically. Bronson came bounding upstairs at the sound, but she seized me more tightly around the neck and held me chokingly. I motioned him back, and succeeded in carrying her away to a quiet place, where I sat down with her in my arms, and made love to her for hours.

I never heard a more pitiful story than she told me, between strangling sobs, of her hungry life. The child has been yearning for affection all the time, but has unconsciously repelled it by her manner. She said nobody on earth loved her except the baby, and now the baby was dead.

"There is no use of your trying to make things different," she said, "especially with mamma. She wouldn't care if I was dead too. But papa could understand, I think, if he would only try to love me. But I love you—oh! I love you so much that it hurts me. Nobody ever came and hugged me up the way you did, in my whole life. You have made things over for me, and I'll love you for it till I die. Why is it that everybody gives mamma and the baby so much love, when they never cared for it, and I care so much and never get a single bit? Nobody understands me, and every one—every one calls me bad. I'm not bad. I love plenty of people who can't love me. I am not bad, I tell you!"

She cried herself nearly sick, and then, exhausted, fell asleep, with her face pressed against mine. Thus Bronson found us. He offered to take her, and I put her into his arms. Then I told him all that she had said, and asked him to hold her until she wakened, and give her some of the love her little heart was hungering for. He couldn't speak when I finished, and I went down, to find Rachel bathing Flossy's head with cologne, and looking worn and tired.

Percival came for Rachel, and one could see that the mere sight of him rested her. She told him all about it, in her wonderfully comprehensive way, and he felt the whole thing, and we were all very quiet and peaceful and sad, as we drove home through the early darkness of that Easter day.

They left me at my door, and I went in alone, with the memory of that grieving household—the lonely father, and the selfish mother, and the unloved child—hallowed and made tender by the presence of the little dead baby, asleep under its weight of violets.

I feel very much alone sometimes; but the Percivals carry their world with them.

VII

A STUDY IN HUMAN GEESE

"I am myself indifferent honest."

I have just made two startling discoveries. One is that I am not honest myself, and the other is that I detest honesty in other people.

To-day I was sitting peacefully in my room, harming nobody, when I saw little Pet Winterbotham drive up in her cart and come running up to the door. I supposed she had come with a message from her sister, and went down, thinking to be detained about ten minutes.

It seems but a few years ago since Pet was in the kindergarten. I was surprised to see that she wore her dresses very long, and that she looked almost grown up.

"My dear Pet," I exclaimed, "what is the matter?"

"Oh, Miss Ruth, I am in such a scrape," she answered me. "I hope you won't think it's queer that I came to you, but the fact is, I've watched you in church, and you always look as if you knew, and would help people if they would ask you to;

so I thought I'd try you.

"Ever and ever so long ago, when I was a little bit of a thing, and played with other children, and you and sister Grace went out together, I used to 'choose' you from all the other young ladies, because you wore such lovely hats, and always had on pearl-colored gloves. I suppose it is so long ago that you were a young lady and had beaux that you've forgotten it. But I know you used to have lovers, for I heard Mrs. Herrick and Mrs. Payson Osborne talking about you once, and Mrs. Herrick said you seemed so tranquil and contented that she supposed you never had had any really good offers, or you would be all the time wishing you had taken one. And Mrs. Osborne spoke up in her quick way, and said, 'Don't deceive yourself so comfortably, my dear Flossy. I know positively that Ruth has had several offers that you and I would have jumped at.' And then she turned away and laughed and laughed, although I didn't see anything so very funny in what she said, and neither did Mrs. Herrick.

"I do think Mrs. Osborne is the loveliest person I know. She is my ideal young married woman. She always has a smile and a pretty word for every one, and young men like her better than they do the buds. Why, your face is as red as fire. I hope I haven't said anything unpleasant. Mamma says I blunder horribly, but she always is too busy to tell me how not to blunder.

"Now, I want to know which of these two men you would advise me to marry. I've got to take one, I suppose."

"Marry!" I exclaimed, so explosively that Pet started. "Why, child, how old are you?"

"I'm nineteen," she said, in rather an injured tone, "and I've always made up my mind to marry young, if I got a good enough offer. I hate old maids. Oh, excuse me. I don't mean you, of course. I wouldn't marry a clerk, you understand, just to be marrying. I'm not so silly. I have plenty of common-sense in other things, and I'm going to put some of it into the marriage question. Don't you think I'm sensible?"

"Very," I answered; but I didn't, Tabby. I thought she was a goose.

"Well now," proceeded my young caller, settling her ribbons with a pretty air of importance, and looking at me out of the most innocent eyes in the world, "my sister Grace married Brian Beck because he had such a lot of money. But you know he is dissipated, and at first Grace almost went distracted. Then she made up her mind to let him go his own gait, and she has as good a time as she can on his money. His Irish name Brian is her thorn in the flesh, and he teases her nearly out of her wits about it. We have great fun on the yacht every summer. Brian is awfully good to me, and invites nice men to take with us; still, much as I like Brian as a brother-in-law, I shouldn't care to have a husband like him. Now, I suppose you wonder why on earth I am telling you these things, and why I don't tell one of the girls I go with."

"Oh, no!" I exclaimed in protest.

"Of course. I see you think it wouldn't be safe. Girls just can't help telling, to save their lives. Sometimes they don't intend to, and then it's bad enough. But sometimes they do it just to be mean, and you can't help yourself. I have plenty of confidence in you though, and you don't look as if you'd be easily shocked. You look as though you could tell a good deal if you wanted to. You're an awfully comfortable sort of a person. Now, let me tell you. I have two offers. One is from Clinton Frost, and the other is from Jack Whitehouse. You have seen me with Mr. Frost, haven't you? A dark, fierce, melancholy man, with black eyes and hair, and very distinguished looking.

"I think he has a history. He throws out hints that way. He is gloomy with everybody but me, and Brian will do nothing but joke with him. There is nothing Mr. Frost dislikes as much as to laugh or to see other people laugh. Brian calls him 'Pet's nightmare,' and threatens to give him ink to drink.

"I believe Mr. Frost hates Brian. He says the name of our yacht, *Hittie Magin*, is unspeakably vulgar. Nothing pleases Brian more than to force Mr. Frost or Grace to tell strangers the name of it. Their mere speaking the words throws Brian into convulsions of laughter. Then, if people comment on it, he tells them that the name is of his wife's selection, in deference to his Irish family. And Grace almost faints with mortification. Mr. Frost says he will give me a yacht twice as good as Brian's. He adores me. He says I am the only thing in life which makes him smile."

I felt that I could sympathize with Mr. Frost on this point.

"Then there's Jack Whitehouse, Norris Whitehouse's nephew. Mr. Norris Whitehouse is a great friend of yours, isn't he? Do you know, I never think of him as an 'eligible,' although he is a bachelor. I should as soon think of a king in that light. He impresses me more than any man I ever knew. Don't you consider him odd? No? I do. He is so clever that you would be afraid of him, if it wasn't for his lovely manners, which make you feel as though what you are saying is just what he has been wanting to know, and he is so glad he has met some one who is able to tell him. Actually he treats me with more respect than some of the young men do. He makes me feel as if I were a woman, and he had a right to expect something good of me. I never said that to anybody before, but I can talk to you and feel that you understand me. I like to feel that

Lilian Bell

people think there is something to me, even if I know that it isn't much. Mrs. Asbury says that Mr. Whitehouse is the courtliest man she knows. You know the story of the Whitehouse money, don't you? Jack told it to me with tears in his eyes, and I don't wonder at it. You know Jack's father and mother died when he was very young. Norris was his father's favorite, and the old gentleman made a most unjust will, leaving only a life interest in the property to Jack's father; then it all went to his favorite younger son, Norris. Now, you know what most men would do under the circumstances. They would acknowledge the injustice of the will, but they would keep the money. This proves to me what an unusual man Mr. Norris Whitehouse is, for he immediately made over to his little nephew Jack one half of the property—just what his father ought to have been able to leave him—and Jack is to come into that when he is twenty-five. Don't you think that was noble? Jack worships him. He says no father could have been more devoted to an only son than his uncle Norris has been to him. He travelled with him, and gave up years of his life to superintending Jack's education.

"Now, whoever marries Jack will really be at the head of that elegant house, for you know it hasn't had a mistress since Jack's mother died, years ago. I should like that, although I do wish more of the expense was in furniture instead of in pictures and tapestries. But that is his uncle's taste.

"Poor Jack talks so beautifully about his young mother, whom he can scarcely remember. He says his uncle has kept her alive to him. He is perfectly lovely with other fellows' mothers, and with mine. He treats them all, he says, as he should like to have had others treat his mother. Of course it is only sentiment with him. If she had lived, he might have given her as much trouble as other boys give theirs. She must have been lovely. Mamma says she was. But I'd just as soon not have any mother-in-law to tell me to wrap up, and wear rubbers if it looked like rain. You know there isn't a bit of sentiment in me. I'm practical. My father says if I had been a boy he would have taken me into business at fifteen. Jack thinks I am all sentiment. He says nobody could have a face like mine and not possess an innate love of the beautiful in art and poetry and all that. I have forgotten just what he said about that part of it. But I know he meant to praise me. I didn't say anything in reply, but I smiled to myself at the idea of Pet Winterbotham being credited with fine sentiment.

"Jack is horribly young—only twenty-two—so he won't have his money for three years, and Mr. Frost is thirty-nine. Jack has curly hair, and when he wears a white tennis suit and puts his cap on the back of his head and holds a cigarette in his hand, he looks as if he had just stepped out of one of the pictures in *Life*. He looks so 'chappie.' He is a good deal easier to get along with than Mr. Frost, and will have more money some day, although Mr. Frost has enough. Now, which would you take?"

"Why, my dear Pet," I said in an unguarded moment, "which do you love?"

I shrivelled visibly under the look of scorn she cast upon me.

"I don't love either of them. I've had one love affair and I don't care for another until I make sure which man I'm going to marry."

"Can you fall in love to order?" I asked in dismay.

"Not exactly. 'To order!' Why, no. Anybody would think you were having boots made. But it's being with a man, and having him awfully good to you, and admiring everything you say, and having lots of good clothes, and not being in love with any other fellow, that makes you love a man. I'm sure from your manner that you like Jack Whitehouse the best, so I think I'll take him. You are awfully sweet, and not a bit like an old maid. I tell everybody so."

"Am I called an Old Maid?" I asked quickly. I could have bitten my tongue out for it afterwards.

"Oh, yes indeed, by all the younger set. You see you belonged to Grace's set and they are all married. It makes you seem like a back number to us, but you don't look like an old maid. I suppose you can look back ages and ages and remember when you had lovers, can't you? Or have you forgotten? I can't imagine you ever getting love-letters or flowers or any such things. I hope I haven't offended you. I am horribly honest, you know. I say just what I think, and you mustn't mind it. Mamma says I am too truthful to be pleasant. But I like honesty myself, don't you?"

And with that, Tabby, she went away.

How terrible the child is! Now, Pet is one of those persons who go about lacerating people and clothing their ignorance, or their insolence, in the garb of honesty.

"I am honest," say they, "so you must not be offended, but is it true that your grandfather was hanged for being a pirate?" Or, "I believe in being perfectly honest with people. How cross-eyed you are!"

This is why honesty is so disreputable. When you say of a woman, "She is one of those honest, outspoken persons," it means that she will probably hurt your feelings, or insult you in your first interview with her.

I don't like to admit it even to you, Tabby, but I am horribly shaken up. After all these years of talking about myself to you as an Old Maid, and knowing that I am one, to hear myself called such, and to catch a glimpse of the way I appear to the oncoming generation, shakes me to the foundation of my being. Soon *I* shall be pushed to the wall, as something too worn out to be needed by bright young people. Soon *I* shall be one of the old people whom I have so dreaded all my life. Dear Tabby-cat! You can remember when Missis received love-letters, can't you? They are not all in the japanned box, are they? Do I seem old to you, kitty? Why, there is actually a tear on your gray fur. Dear me, what a silly Old Maid Missis is!

You see, after all, I have not been honest, even with myself. And, just between you and me, I will say that I abominate honesty in other people. There!

VIII

A GAME OF HEARTS

"Man proposes, but Heaven disposes."

Tabby, did you ever hear me speak of Charlie Hardy? No, of course not. Your mother must have been a kitten when I knew Charlie the best. He is a nice boy. Boy! What am I talking about? He is as old as I am. But he is the kind of man who always seems a boy, and everybody who has known him two days calls him Charlie.

Rachel Percival never thought much of him. She said he was weak, and weakness in a man is something Rachel never excuses. She says it is trespassing on one of the special privileges of our sex. Thus she disposed of Charlie Hardy.

"Look at his chin," said Rachel; "could a man be strong with a chin like that?"

"But he is so kind-hearted and easy to get along with," I urged.

"Very likely. He hasn't strength of mind to quarrel. He is unwilling, like most easy-going men, to inflict that kind of pain. But he could be as cruel as the grave in other ways. Look at him. He always is in hot water about something, and never does as people expect him to do."

"But he doesn't do wrong on purpose, and he makes charming excuses and apologies."

"He ought to; he has had enough practice," answered Rachel, with her beautiful smile. "He has what I call a conscience for surface things. He regards life from the wrong point of view, and, as to his always intending to do right—you know the place said to be paved with good intentions. No, no, Ruth. Charlie Hardy is a dangerous man, because he is weak. Through such men as he comes very bitter sorrow in this world."

That conversation, Tabby, took place, if not before you were created, at least in your early infancy—the time when your own weight threw you down if you tried to walk, and when ears and tail were the least of your make-up.

All these years Charlie has never married, but was always with the girls. He dropped with perfect composure from our set to Sallie Cox's—was her slave for two years, though Sallie declares that she never was engaged to him. "What's the use of being engaged to a man that you can keep on hand without?" quoth Sallie. But Charlie bore no malice. "I didn't stand the ghost of a show with a girl like Sallie, when she had such men as Winston Percival and those literary chaps around her. It was great sport to watch her with those men. You know what a little chatterbox she is. By Jove! when that fellow Percival began to talk, Sallie never had a word to say for herself. It must have been awfully hard for her, but she certainly let him do all the talking, and just sat and listened, looking as sweet as a peach. Oh! I never had any chance with Sallie."

Nevertheless, he was usher at her wedding, then dropped peacefully to the next younger set, and now is going with girls of Pet Winterbotham's age.

I thoroughly like the boy, but I can't imagine myself falling in love with him. If I were married to another man—an indiscreet thing for an Old Maid to say, Tabby, but I only use it for illustration—I should not mind Charlie Hardy's dropping in for Sunday dinner every week, if he wanted to. He never bothers. He never is in the way. He is as deft at buttoning a glove as he is amiable at playing cards. You always think of Charlie Hardy first if you are making up a theatre party. He serves equally well as groomsman or pall-bearer—although I do not speak from experience in either instance. He never is cross or sulky. He makes the best of everything, and I think men say that he is "an all-round good fellow."

I depend a great deal upon other men's opinion of a man. I never thoroughly trust a man who is not a favorite with his own sex. I wish men were as generous to us in that respect, for a woman whom other women do not like is just as dangerous. And I never knew simple jealousy—the reason men urge against accepting our verdict—to be universal enough to condemn a woman. There always are a few fair-minded women in every community—just enough to be in the minority—to break continuous jealousy.

Be that as it may, the man I am talking about has kept up his acquaintance with Rachel and Alice Asbury and me in a desultory way, and occasionally he grows confidential. The last time I saw him he said:

"Sometimes I wish I were a woman, Ruth, when I get into so much trouble with the girls. Women never seem to have any worry over love affairs. All they have to do is to lean back and let men wait on them until they see one that suits them. It is like ordering from a *menu* card for them to select husbands. You run over a list for a girl—oysters, clams, or terrapin—and she takes terrapin. In the other case she runs over her own list—Smith, Jones, or Robinson—and likewise takes the rarest. But she is not at all troubled about it. Marrying is so easy for a girl. It comes natural to her."

Tabby, I did wish that he knew as much of the internal mechanism of the engagements that you and I have participated in, by proxy, as we do—if he would understand, profit by, and speedily forget the knowledge.

But, like the hypocrite I am, I only smiled indulgently at him, as if, for women, marrying was mere reposing on eider-down cushions, with the tiller ropes in their hands, while men did the rowing. I was not going to admit, Tabby, that the most of the girls we know never worked harder in their lives than during that indefinite and mysterious period known as "making up their minds." You see I uphold my own sex at all hazards—to men.

He was standing up to go when he said that, but there was something about him which led me to suspect that he was in a condition when he needed some woman to straighten out his affairs. I made no reply, which threw the burden of continuing the conversation upon him. I was in that passive state which made me perfectly willing to have him say good-night and go home or stay and confess to me, just as he chose. I knew he needed me; a good many men need their mothers once in a while as much as they ever did when boys. There was something whimsically boyish about Charlie as he leaned over the back of a tall chair and debated secretly whether or not he should confide in me.

"Why don't you ask me why I said that?" he said.

"Because I know without asking. You were induced to say it by what you have been thinking of all the evening. It sounded like a beginning, but really it was an ending."

He looked as though he thought me a mind-reader, but I fancy the knack of divining when people need a confidant is preternaturally developed in old maids.

"How good you are, Ruth."

"You men always think women are good when they understand you. But it isn't goodness."

"No, you're right. It's more comfortable than goodness. It's odd how you do it. May I tell you about it? You won't think half as well of me as you do now, but it needs just such women as you to keep men straight, and if you will give me your opinion I vow I'll do as you say, even if it kills me."

I was afraid from that desperate ending that it was something serious, and it was. He made several attempts before he could begin. Finally he burst out with,

"Although you are the easiest person in the world to talk to, and I've known you always, it is pretty hard to lay this case before you so that you won't think me a conceited prig. That is because you are a woman and can't help looking at it from a woman's standpoint. For a good many reasons it would be easier to tell it to some man, who would know how it was himself; but you see I want a woman's conscience and a woman's judgment, because you can put yourself in another woman's place."

He grew quite red as he talked, and I waited patiently for him to go on, but gave him no help.

"Well, here goes. If you hate me afterwards I can't help it. I had no idea it would be so hard to tell you or I shouldn't have attempted it. But since you have been sitting there looking at me I am beginning to think differently of it myself, and I'm sure that, with all your kindness, you will be very hard on me, and tell me to accept the hardest alternative. Now, Ruth, you'd better shake hands with me and say good-by while you like me, because you will think of me as another Charlie Hardy when I've finished."

He actually held out his hand, but I folded mine together.

"No," I said, smiling, "I shall not bid you good-by until I really am through with you. Don't look so discouraged. Come; possibly I may be a better friend to you than you think."

"You are awfully good," he said again. I don't know when I have so impressed a man with my extraordinary goodness as I did by listening to Charlie while he did all the talking. If I could have held my tongue another hour, he would have called me an angel.

"Well, although you may not know it, I am engaged to Louise King. I always have been very fond of her, and when I found I couldn't get Sallie, I was sure I cared as much for Louise as I ever could care for anybody, and I was perfectly satisfied with her—thought she would make me an awfully good wife, and all that. But while Miss Taliaferro was up here visiting Sallie, I was with her a good deal, and the first thing I knew we were dead in love with each other. You know we were both in Sallie's wedding-party, and I tell you, Ruth, to stand up at the altar with a girl he is already half in love with, plays the very deuce with a man. Kentucky girls are all pretty, I suppose—everybody says so, and you have to make believe you think so whether you do or not; but this one—you know her? Isn't she the prettiest thing you ever saw? Well, of course she didn't know I was engaged, and I kept putting off telling her, until the first thing I knew I was letting her see how much I thought of her. I don't suppose it was at all difficult to see, but girls are keen on such subjects, and a man can't be in love with one more than a week before she knows more about it than he does. Then, after she told me that she loved me, how could I tell her that, in spite of what I had said, I was engaged to another girl? Wouldn't she have thought I was a rascal? No; I had to let her go home thinking that, if we were not already engaged, we should be some time, and I went part way with her, and—it was a mean trick to play, but the nonsensical things that unthinking people do precipitate affairs which perhaps without their means might never fully develop. Brian Beck heard that I was going a few miles with her, and he and Sallie and Payson came down to the train to see us off. Just as we pulled out of the station, Brian made the most frantic signs for me to open the window, and when I did so, he threw a tissue-paper package at me. Frankie and I both made an effort to catch it. Of course it burst when we touched it, and a good pound of rice was scattered all over us. You never saw such a sight. It flew in every direction; her hat and my hair were full of it. Some went down my collar. Of course everybody in the car roared and—well, I'm not done blushing at it yet. Frankie took it much better than I, and only laughed at it. But I—I felt more like crying. I saw instantly how it complicated things. It was a nail driven into my coffin.

"We had no more than settled down from that and were just having a good little talk, after the passengers had stopped looking at us, when the porter appeared, bringing a basket of white flowers with two turtle-doves suspended from the handle, and Brian Beck's card on it. I wish you could have heard the people laugh. I declare to you, Ruth, when I saw that great white thing coming and knew what it meant, it looked as big as a billiard-table to me. I was going to pay the fellow to take it out again, but no—Frankie wanted it. She made me put it down on the opposite seat and there it stood. Those sickening birds were too much for me, so I jerked them off and threw them out of the window, conscious that my face was very red and that I was amusing more people than I had bargained for.

"When the time came for me to get off and take the train back, Frankie implored me to go on with her, urging how strange it would look to people, who all thought we were married, to see me disappear and have her go on alone. I railed at the idea, but she was in earnest, and when I told her positively that I couldn't—thinking more, I must admit, of the state of my affairs than of hers—she began to cry under her veil. That settled it. Of course I couldn't stand it to see the girl I loved cry, so I went home with her, fell deeper in love every minute I was there, and came away feeling like a cur because I had not spoken to her father. Her people met me in the cordial, honest manner of those who have faith in mankind, but I couldn't look them in the face without flinching.

"Since I came back, of course, I've been visiting Louise as usual. I told her all about the rice and flowers, thinking that if she quarrelled with me about the affair she would break off the engagement. But she only laughed and said it served me right for flirting with every girl that came along, and didn't even reproach me. She has absolute faith in me. She doesn't believe I could sink so low as I have, any more than she could. She has idealized me until I don't dare to breathe for fear of destroying the illusion. She thinks that I love her in the way she loves me, but I couldn't. It isn't in me, Ruth. I don't even love Frankie that way. To tell the truth, Louise is too good for me. She is magnificent, but I am rather afraid of

Lilian Bell

her. She has so many ideals and is so intense. Her faith in me makes me shiver. I am not a bit comfortable with her. I do not even understand how she can love me so much. I am nothing extraordinary, but if you knew the way she treats me, you would think I was Achilles or some of those Greek fellows. She has refused better and richer men than I. Norris Whitehouse has loved her all her life, and you know what a splendid man he is, but Louise ridicules the idea of ever caring for anybody but me. She is so perfect that there is absolutely no flaw in her for me to recognize and feel friendly with. She reads me like a book, but I am less acquainted with her than I was before we were engaged. She says such beautiful things to me sometimes, things that are far beyond my comprehension, and she can get so uplifted that I feel as if I never had met her. There's no use in talking; after a girl falls in love with a man she often ceases to be the girl he courted."

I recalled what I had said to Percival—"Often a woman denies herself the expression of the best part of her love, for fear that it will be either a puzzle or a terror to her lover." Such a saying belonged to Percival. I shouldn't think of repeating it to Charlie, for he could not comprehend it. I should puzzle him as much as Louise did. It made me heartsick. How could even Charlie Hardy so persistently misunderstand the grandeur of Louise King? Yet how could such a glorious girl imagine herself in love with nice, weak, agreeable Charlie Hardy?

Louise is a younger, handsomer, more impetuous, less clever edition of Rachel Percival; but she is of that order. She is less concentrated and more emotional than Rachel. I did not quite know how a great sorrow would affect Louise. Rachel would use it as a stepping-stone towards heaven.

I have seen a young, untried race-horse with small, pointed, restless ears; with delicate nostrils where the red blood showed; with full, soft eyes where fire flashed; with a satin skin so thin and glossy that even the lightest hand would cause it to quiver to the touch; where pride and fire and royal blood seemed to urge a trial of their powers; and I have thought: "You are capable of passing anything on the track and coming under the wire triumphant and victorious; or you might fulfil your prophecy equally well by falling dead in your first heat, with the red blood gushing from those thin nostrils. We can be sure of nothing until you are tried, but it is a quivering delight to look at you and to share your impatience and to wonder what you will do."

Occasionally I see women who affect me in the same way—idealists, capable of being wounded through their sensitiveness by things which we ordinary mortals accept philosophically; capable also of greater heights of happiness and lower depths of misery, but of suffering most through being misunderstood. To this class Rachel and Louise belong. Rachel, in Percival, has reached a haven where she rides at anchor, sheltered from such storms as had hitherto almost engulfed her, and growing more heroically beautiful in character day by day. Poor Louise is still at sea, with a great storm brewing. How hard, how terribly hard, to talk to Charlie Hardy about her, when, after the solemnity of an engagement tie between them, he was capable of misunderstanding, not only her, but the whole situation so blindly! But what a calamity it would be if Louise should marry him!

"Go on, Ruth. Say something, do. I imagine all sorts of things while you just sit there looking at me so solemnly. I realize that I am in a tight place. I did hope that you could see some way out of it for me; but I know, by the way you act, that you think I ought to give up Frankie—dear little girl!—and marry Louise, and by Jove! if you say it's the handsome thing to do, I'll do it."

This still more effectually closed my lips. He so evidently thought that he was being heroic. He added rather reluctantly, "I must say that I suppose Frankie Taliaferro would get over it much more easily than Louise could."

"Charlie," I said slowly, "you don't mean to be, but you are too conceited to live. I wonder that you haven't died of conceit before this."

Charlie's blond face flushed and he looked deeply offended.

"Conceited!" he burst out. "Why, Ruth, there isn't a fellow going who has a worse opinion of himself than I have. I don't see what either of those girls sees in me to love, I tell you. I am not proud of it. I wish to Heaven they didn't love me. *I* haven't made them."

"'Haven't made them'! Yes, you have. You are just the kind of man who does. You say pretty things even to old women, and bring them shawls and put footstools under their feet with the air of a lover. And if you only hand a woman an ice you look unutterable things. You have a dozen girls at a time in that indefinite state when three words to any one of them would engage you to her, and she would think you had deliberately led up to it; whereas all the past had been idle admiration on your part, and it was a rose in her hair or a moment in the conservatory that upset you, and there you are. Oh, these girls, these girls, who believe every time a man at a ball says he loves them that he means it! Why can't you be satisfied to have some of them friends, and not all sweethearts?"

"It can't be done. I've tried and I know. Sallie tried it and it married her off—a thing not one of her flirtations could have accomplished. This is the way it goes. You arrange with a girl not to have any nonsense, but just to be good friends.

You take her to the theatre, drive with her, dance with her. Soon her chaperon begins to eye you over. Fellows at the club drop a remark now and then. You explain that you are only friends, and they wink at you and you feel foolish. Next time they see you with her, they look knowing, and you see, to your horror, that the girl is blushing. Evidently she is under fire too. Still, you keep it up. She makes a better comrade than any of the men. You feel that you are out of mischief when you are with her. She keeps you alert. You never are bored, but really you are not as fond of her as you were of your college chum even. She treats you a trifle, just a trifle, differently from all the other men. This goes to your head. You begin to make a little difference yourself. You take her hand when you say good-night, just as you would one of the men. But it is not the same. The girl has needles or electricity in her hand. You can't let go. You begin to feel that friendship, too, can be dangerous. Next day you send her flowers, with some lines about the delights of friendship. She accepts both beautifully, but you have a guilty feeling that you did it to remind her. She does not seem to understand that there had been any necessity. Still, you feel rather mean, and to make up for it you try to atone by your manner. She is looking perfectly lovely. She wears white. You particularly like white. She knows it. You think perhaps she wore it to please you. *How* pretty she is! You lose your head a little and say something. She looks innocent and surprised. She 'thought we were just friends. Surely,' she says, 'you have said so often enough. Why change? Friends are so much more comfortable.' She wants to 'stay a friend.' You are miserable at the idea, although that morning it was just what you wanted. You were even afraid she would think differently. What an ass a man can be! You fling discretion to the winds and tell her—you tell her—well, you go home engaged to her. That's how a friendship ends. Bah!"

"A realistic recital. From hearsay, of course! The next day

Lilian Bell

the man wishes he were well out of it, I suppose?"

"Not quite so soon as that, but soon enough."

"Ah, I wish you knew, Charlie Hardy, how all this sounds even to such a good friend of yours as I am. It is such men as you who lower the standard of love and of men in general. Do you suppose a girl who has had an encounter with you, and seen how trifling you are, can have her first beautiful faith to give to the truly grand hero when he comes? No; it has been bruised and beaten down by what you call 'a little flirtation,' and possibly her unwillingness to trust a second time may force her true lover into withdrawing his suit. How dare men and women trifle with the Shekinah of their lives? And when it has been dulled by abuse, what a pitiful Shekinah it appears to the one who approaches it reverently, confidently expecting it to be the uncontaminated holy of holies! It is this sort of thing which makes infidels about love."

Charlie began to look sulky, feeling, I suppose, that I was piling the sins of the universe on to his already burdened shoulders.

"I dare say you are right, but what am I to do?"

"There is only one thing for you to do, but I know you won't do it."

"Yes, I will. Only try me," he said, brightening up.

"You must go and tell Louise that you are in love with Frankie Taliaferro."

"Tell Louise? Why, Ruth, it would kill her. You don't know her. She wouldn't let me off. You don't know how a girl in love feels. Ruth, were you ever in love?"

"That is not a pertinent question," I said. "It comes quite near being the other thing. But let me tell you, Charlie Hardy, I know Louise King, and it won't kill her. You know 'men have died and worms have eaten them, but not for love.' That might be said of women." (I didn't know, Tabby, whether it might or might not. I couldn't afford to let him see my doubts, if I had any.) "We don't die as easily as you men seem to think."

"But is this your view of what is right?" he asked. "I was sure you would counsel the other. I've been fortifying myself to give Frankie up and marry Louise, and, with all due respect to you, I must say that I think you are wrong here. You must remember that my honor is involved."

"Bother your honor!" I cried explosively. Charlie seemed rather pleased than otherwise at my inelegance. "I am tired to death of hearing men fall back on nonsense about their honor. I notice they seldom feel called upon to refer to it unless they are involved in something disreputable."

Charlie straightened up at this and settled his coat with an indignant jerk.

"I hardly think," he began stiffly, "that I am involved in anything disreputable in being engaged to Miss King."

"What are a man's debts of honor?" I went on with growing excitement. "Gaming debts and things he would scarcely care to explain to the public at large. Your honor is involved in this, is it? And you must save your honor at all hazards, no matter who goes to the wall in the process! I suppose if you made the rash vow that, if your horse won the race, you would cut your mother's head off, while you were still in the flush of victory, you would seize your bowie-knife and go to work! No? Oh, yes, Charlie. Your honor, as you call it, is involved. I insist upon it. You must do it. Oh, I am going too far, am I? Not one step further than men go in the mire whither their honor leads them. Debts of honor, indeed! Debts of dishonor I call them. So do most women."

"Yes, but, Ruth," interrupted Charlie uneasily, "an engagement is different. I don't dispute what you say in regard to gambling debts—"

"You can't," I murmured rebelliously.

"—but a man can't, with any decency, ask a girl to release him when he has sought her out and asked her to marry him."

"Perhaps not with decency. But it is a place where this precious honor of yours might come into play. It would at least be honorable."

"There isn't a man who would agree with you," he cried.

"Nor is there a woman who would agree with you," I retorted. But both of us stretched things a little at this point.

He thought over the situation for a few minutes, then said,

"You understand that, in my opinion, Louise loves me the best."

"The best—yes. For that very reason you must not marry her. O Charlie! try to understand," I pleaded. "She must love the best when she loves at all. She has loved the best in you, until she has put it out of your reach ever to attain to it. It would not be fair to the girl, it would be robbing her, to accept all this beautiful love for you, and give her in return—

your love for another girl. Do you suppose for an instant that you could continue to deceive her after you were married? Supposing she found out afterwards, then what? She might die of that. I cannot say. It would be enough to kill her. But not if you are honest and manly enough to tell her in time to save her self-respect. You are powerless to touch it now. You could kill it if you were married."

"Honest and manly enough to confess myself a rascal? I don't see where it would come in," he replied gloomily.

"It is the nearest approach to it which lies in your power."

"If the girls' places were only reversed now! I could tell Frankie that I had been false to our engagement and had fallen in love with Louise. She would know how it was herself. But Louise couldn't comprehend such things. I believe she has been as true to me, even in thought, as if she had been my wife. How can I tell her?"

"The more you say, the plainer you make it your duty. I say, how can you not tell her?"

"I might go away for a year and not let her know and not write to her. Then she would know without my having to tell her."

"You wouldn't stand it if a man called you a coward. Don't try my woman's friendship for you too far. You insult me by offering such a suggestion."

"Gently, gently, Ruth. I beg your pardon." (Rachel was right in saying he would not quarrel. I wished he would. I never wanted to quarrel so much in my life.)

"I am a coward," he broke down at last. "I'll spare you the

trouble of saying so. But oh, Ruth, you don't know how I dread a scene! You go and tell her. I can't. I couldn't even write it."

"How unselfish you are! Spare yourself at all hazards, Charlie, for of course it was not your fault that things got into such a state."

"Oh, Ruth, don't!"

"Well, I won't. But do you realize how I should insult her if I went to her? It's bad enough for you, the man she loves, to tell her. From any one else it would be unforgivable. Do as you like. You promised to follow my advice. Take it and do as you will with it. But I will guarantee the result if you will do as I say. Come, Charlie. One hour, and it will all be over, and you can marry Frankie."

It was like getting him into a dentist's chair. I felt a wholesome self-contempt as I thus sugar-coated his pill, but he was so abject in his misery.

Charlie brightened up perceptibly at the alluring prospect. He shut his eyes to the dark path which led to happiness, and was revelling in its glory.

"Ruth, you dear thing! I don't see how I ever can thank you enough," he said, taking both my hands in his. "I ought to have stuck to you, that's what I ought to have done. You would have kept me straight. Do you know, I used to be awfully in love with you. You really were my first love. I was about eighteen then. You don't look a day older, and you are just as sweet as ever."

I laughed outright.

"What did I tell you?" I cried. "You can't help making love to save your life. Your gratitude is getting you into deeper water every minute. Go home, do. Run for your life, or you'll be engaged to me too. *Then* who'll help you out?"

He acted upon my suggestion and went hastily.

Tabby, did you ever? He never was in love with me, never on this earth. Whatever possessed him to say such a thing? He loses his head, that's what he does. I hope he won't meet any woman younger than his grandmother before he gets home, or he might propose to her.

* * * * *

My heart stands still when I think of Louise King.

IX

THE MADONNA OF THE QUIET MIND

"It is not true that love makes all things easy, but it makes us   choose what is difficult."

Across the street, in plain view from my window, has come to dwell a little brown wren of a woman with her five babies. The house, hitherto inconspicuous among its finer neighbors, at the advent of the Mayo family suddenly bloomed into a home. The lawn blossomed with living flowers and the windows framed faces which shamed, in their dimpling loveliness, the painted cherubs on the wall.

It was a delight to see Nellie Mayo in the midst of her children. Hers were all babies, such dear, amiable, kissable babies, each of whom seemed personally anxious to prove to every one how much sweetness one small morsel of humanity could hold. But with five of them, bless me! the house was one glowing radiance of sunshine, in which the little mother lived and loved, until they absorbed each other's personality, and it was difficult to think of one without the others.

Sometimes in a street-car or on the elevated train I have seen women who I felt convinced had little babies at home. It is because of the peculiar look they wear, the rapturous mother-look, which has its home in the eyes during the most helpless period of babyhood—an indescribable look, in which dreams and prophecy and heaven are mingled. It is the sweetest look which can come to a woman's face, saying plainly, "Oh, I have such a secret in my heart! Would that every one knew its rapture with me!" It wears off sooner or later, but with Nellie Mayo, whether because there always was a baby, or because each was welcomed with such a world of love, the look remained until it seemed a part of her face.

Long ago we knew her as an unworldly girl, whose peachblow coloring gave to her face its chief beauty, although her plaintive blue eyes and smooth brown hair called forth a certain protective faith in her simplicity and goodness. Sometimes girlhood is a mysterious chaos of traits, out of which no one can foretell what sort of cosmos will follow, or whether there will be a cosmos at all or only intelligent chaos to the end. But this girl seemed to carry her future in her face. She was a little mother to us all. It was a tribute to her gentleness and dignity that, although she was a poor girl among a bevy of rich ones, she was a favorite; unacknowledged perhaps, but still a favorite. She always stood ready with her unostentatious help. She was every-body's understudy. Flossy Carleton, as she was then, fastened herself like a leech upon Nellie's capacity for aid, and was a likely subject for the exercise of Nellie's swifter brain and willing feet; for to see any one's unspoken need was to her like a thrilling cry for help, and was the only thing which could completely draw her from her shy reserve. The chief reason she was popular was that she had a faculty of keeping herself in the shadow. You never knew where she was until you wanted her, when she would seem to rise out of the earth to your side. But, in spite of your intense gratitude at the moment, you really found yourself taking her as a matter of course. She was one of those who are fully appreciated only when they are dead, and who then call forth the bitterest remorse that we have not made them know in life how dear they were and how painfully necessary to our happiness.

It is rather a sad commentary upon those same girls, who accepted Nellie's assistance most readily, to record that, when they were launched into society and were deep in the mysteries of full-fledged young-ladyhood, little Nellie Maddox was seldom invited to their most fashionable gatherings, but came in, at first, before their memory grew too rusty, for the simpler luncheons and teas.

This is not a history of intentional or systematic neglect, but a mere statement of the way things drifted along. Not one of the girls would wilfully have omitted her, if she had been in the habit of being asked; but it was easy to let her name slip when all the rest did it, and so gradually it came to pass that we seldom saw her. Then she married Frank Mayo, who would not be offended if he heard a newsboy refer to him as "a gent," or a maid-servant describe him as "a pretty man." Of such a one it is scarcely necessary to add that he was selfish, inordinately conceited, and, to complete the description, a trifle vulgar. He never suspected his wife's cleverness nor appreciated her worship. It almost made me doubt her cleverness to see how she idolized him, but this instance went far towards proving that love, with some women, is entirely an affair of the heart. It irritates Rachel to hear any one say so. She says it argues ignorance of a nice distinction in terms, and that when the brain is not concerned it should be called by a baser name.

I doubt if she could have brought herself to say so if she had been looking into Nellie Mayo's blue eyes, which looked tired and a little less blue than as I remembered them. They had pathetic purple shadows under them, which told of sleepless nights with the babies, and there were fine lines around her mouth; but her light-brown hair was as smooth and her dress as plain and neat as ever.

It was like watching a nest of birds. I felt my own love expand to see the wealth of affection Nellie had for her precious family. Her unselfish zeal never flagged. She flitted from one want to another as naturally as she breathed and with as little consciousness of the process. Her household machinery ran no more smoothly than many another's, but Nellie met and surmounted all obstacles with an unruffled brow. Her outward calm was the result of some great inward peace. She simply had developed naturally from the girl we had known before we grew up and went away to be "finished by travel."

Nothing could go so wrongly, no nerves throb so pitilessly, that they prevented her meeting her husband with the smile reserved for him alone. None of the babies could call it forth. When he came home tired, Nellie fluttered around him making him comfortable, as if life held for her no sweeter task.

Being a woman myself, and having no husband to wait upon until it became natural, I used to feel somewhat vexed that he never served her, instead of receiving the best of everything so complacently. He never seemed to realize that she might be tired or needed a change of routine. That household revolved around him. Of course it was partly Nellie's fault that he had fallen into the habit of receiving everything and making no return. Fallen into it? No. With that kind of a man, an only son, and considered by the undiscriminating to be good-looking, his wife had only to take up his mother's unfinished work of spoiling him. It is true that these unselfish women inculcate a system of selfishness in their families which often works their ruin. They rob the children

Lilian Bell

of their rightful virtue of self-sacrifice.

So Nellie idolized her husband. He was her king, and the king could do no wrong. She taught the babies a sweet system of idolatry, which so far had been harmless. He cared very little for children; so, when yearning to express their love for the hero of all their mother's stories, with their little hearts almost bursting with affection, their love was most frequently tested by being obliged to keep away from their idol in order "not to bother him" with their kisses. Fortunately these same withheld kisses were dear to Nellie, and she never was too busy to accept and return them. Thus they never knew how busy she was. She was sure to be about some sweet task for others. If she ever rested, it was with the cosiest corner occupied by somebody else.

I wonder what will happen when, in heaven, one of these selfless mothers is led in triumph to a solid gold throne, all lined with eider-down cushions, where she can take the rest she never had on earth. Won't she stagger back against the glittering walls of the New Jerusalem and say, "Not for me. Not for me. Surely it must be for my husband?" But there, where places are appointed, she will not be allowed to give it up—which may make her miserable even in heaven. Ah me, these mothers! It brings tears to my eyes to think of their unending love, which wraps around and shelters and broods over every one, whose helplessness clings to their help, whose need depends upon their exhaustless supply. Theirs it is to bear the invisible but princely crest, "Ich dien."

Nellie had no time for literary classes. Her music, of which we used to predict great things, had resolved itself into lullabies and kindergarten ditties for the children. She seldom found an opportunity to visit even me. So it was I who went there and saw how her life was literally bound by the four walls of that little brown house; yet I never felt any inclination to pity her, because she was so contented. I knew of others who seemed happier—that is, the word seemed to describe them better—but none of them possessed Nellie Mayo's placid content.

Still, I did not like her husband. He was not of Nellie's fine fibre. He was dull, while she was delightfully clever. His eyes were rather good, but he had a way of throwing expressive glances at me, as he talked upon trifling subjects, which disgusted me. I reluctantly made up my mind that he considered himself a "lady-killer," but I felt outraged that he should waste his ammunition upon me. I tried to be amused by it, when I found indignation was useless with him. I used to call him "Simon Tappertit" to myself, until I once forgot and referred to him as "Simon" before Nellie, when I gave up being amused and let it bore me naturally. I always had treated him with unusual consideration for Nellie's sake, and even had tried genuinely to admire him because it gave her such pleasure; but when I discovered that the jackanapes took it as an evidence that he was progressing in my esteem, I did not know whether to laugh or cry with vexation.

All at once, without any explanation or preface, Sallie began calling upon Mrs. Mayo and sending her flowers from her conservatories. Often when Sallie came to see me her coachman had orders to be at Mrs. Mayo's disposal, to take the children for a drive, while Sallie and I sat and talked about everything except why she had embarked upon this venture. I was sure there was something in it which must be kept out of sight, because Sallie never would talk about them.

I noticed that whenever Frank was away from home—which grew more and more frequent—an invitation was sure to come for the Mayos from Sallie. But Nellie never accepted without him, whether from pride or timidity I could not then determine, and all Sallie's efforts to persuade her were unavailing.

It was such an unusual proceeding in Mrs. Payson Osborne to seek out any one that it excited my wonder. But she was not to be balked by anything; moreover, I had great faith in her motives, which were sound and good, even if her plans of carrying them out inclined to the frivolous.

But all at once her frivolity seemed to reach a climax. She issued invitations for a lawn fete, to be followed by a very private, very select dinner, after which came the cotillon. She had decorators from New York, and otherwise ordered the most extravagant setting for her entertainment. This might not seem unusual to every one, but with us, who are accustomed to extracting our enjoyment from one party at a time, this seemed rather a superb affair. Pet Winterbotham was almost wild with delight.

"Only think," she cried, "she has asked Jack and me to lead the cotillon! Isn't that sweet of her? Oh, I do think she is the dearest thing! Though I must say I'd rather have been asked to the dinner. That's going to be perfectly elegant. I heard it was to be given for somebody, but I don't know who it could be. It might be for Frankie Taliaferro. Mrs. Osborne has asked her to come up for it."

Pet's remarks rushed on until I soon found myself carried along the tide of her enthusiasm, which she assured me was shared by every girl in town.

I shall not attempt to describe Sallie's success. The weather, the people, fortune itself, was in her favor, and the whole afternoon was admirable. I confess, however, that it was with some slight curiosity that I awaited the dinner.

Sallie's cheeks were flushed and her eyes shone with an unusual brilliancy as she greeted us, but the proverbial feather would have felled any one of her guests when Payson offered his arm to Mrs. Frank Mayo, who rose out of a shadowy corner in a high-throated gown and led us to the dining-room. I caught Sallie's eye as she laid her hand on Frank Mayo's arm, and she gave me a comical look, half imploring, half defiant.

I was guilty of wondering if Sallie had been demented when she planned that dinner-table, for this is the way we found ourselves:

Next to Frank Mayo came Alice Asbury, encased in freezing dignity. Brian Beck, at his worst, supported her on the other hand. After Brian were Louise King and Charlie Hardy, both looking to my practised eyes exceedingly stiff and uncomfortable. I had no time to wonder if the blow had fallen, in casting a glance at the other guests. Nellie Mayo was admirably situated between Charlie Hardy and Payson Osborne, both of whom were deference itself to her. The difference in her simple attire from the full dress all around her in no wise disturbed her unworldly spirit. She looked with quiet admiration at the handsome shoulders of Louise and Rachel, evidently never dreaming that the babies' mother might be expected to follow their example in dress.

Grace Beck, sitting by Norris Whitehouse, would have an excellent opportunity of cementing or breaking off the prospective match, which as yet was unannounced, between her sister and his nephew. Rachel would be polite, but not wildly entertaining, to Asbury; but he could count on me to be decent to him, while I snatched crumbs of intellectual comfort from Percival on my other hand. But Sallie had placed the funereal Clinton Frost between that rattle-pated Frankie Taliaferro and her lively self, probably with the

Lilian Bell

laudable intention of seeing whether his face would be permanently disfigured by a smile. Nor was the poor wretch out of Brian Beck's reach, but was made the objective point of Brian's liveliest sallies, the hero of his most piquant and impossible stories, which convulsed us until I felt sure that the irritated Mr. Frost must cherish a secret but lively desire to punch his head. Possibly Brian was the only one who thoroughly enjoyed himself at that ill-starred dinner, for he is keen on the scent of a precarious situation which is liable to involve everybody in total collapse. In this instance he seemed to snuff the battle from afar and stirred up all the slumbering elements of discord with unctuous satisfaction; and if it had not been for the wicked twinkle in his Irish blue eyes, which none of his victims could withstand, it might have resulted seriously. He gayly rallied Charlie Hardy on his flirtations; predicted seeing him yet brought up with a round turn in a breach-of-promise case; seemed highly edified by Frankie Taliaferro's efforts to appear unconcerned at these pleasantries; railed openly at Clinton Frost's being so unresponsive to the general mirth around him; shivered visibly at that gentleman's icy retorts; playfully called attention to his wife's endeavors to frown him into silence; and, in spite of Sallie's angry glances, really saved her dinner from proving a dismal failure. Indeed, the cases were too real, and too much genuine misery was concealed behind impassive faces, not to prove a dangerous situation, the tension of which was relieved by Brian's extravagant nonsense. Percival and Norris Whitehouse were sincerely amused by the wit in which Brian clothed his droll remarks. But the greatest misfortune of the dinner-giver was realized in Frank Mayo, the man who thinks he can tell a good story. The Mayos were so new to all of us that this peculiarity was not suspected until Brian discovered it and dragged it forth. He persuaded Frank to talk, listened with absorbing interest to the flattest tales, encouraged him if he flagged, and laughed until the tears came if he by chance forgot or slurred a point.

However, no one seemed to think that there was anything seriously amiss except Sallie, who is a human barometer when she has guests. She knows by instinct when they are or are not being entertained. Nor was her tact at fault in seating the people, for I was the only one laden with almost unbearable knowledge, and I fell asleep that night thinking that possibly the situation was not so unusual as it appeared to me. I dare say plenty of dinners are given with just as many unsuspected trap-doors to sensationalism.

Lilian Bell

X

THE PATHOS OF FAITH

"To him who is shod the whole world is covered with leather."

The next afternoon I was resting and thinking over the brilliancy of the Payson Osborne entertainment, when Sallie came in, dressed from head to foot in black. There was not a suspicion of white at wrist or throat. I was too startled to ask a question until her burst of laughter relieved me.

"You poor thing!" she cried, "did I frighten you? But I *am* in mourning; yes, truly, for my dinner-party. Ruth, Ruth, what was the matter with it?"

"Why, nothing. It was exquisitely served, and oh, Sallie, your lawn fete and the cotillon were beautiful. They were perfect. Truly, you do give the most successful entertainments in town."

"Certainly—why shouldn't I," said Sallie sharply, "when I have never done anything, *anything* all my life but go to parties and study how to give them? Oh, Ruth, dear, I do get so tired of it all. But," taking on a brisker tone, "all the more reason why I should never give such a sad affair as that dinner. That dinner, Ruth, was what Brian Beck calls a howling failure. Payson never criticises anything that I do, but even he came to me quite gingerly this morning, after I had read what the papers had to say about it, and said, 'My dear child, what was the matter with your tea-party?' Now, let us admit the success of the other two, and weep a little in a friendly way over the 'tea-party.'"

"I had a lovely time—" I began, but Sallie interrupted me.

"Hypocrite!" she cried vehemently. "You know you didn't. Your eyes were as big as turkey platters with apprehension."

"My dear Sallie," I expostulated.

"Don't you dare put on airs with me, then," she said mutinously. "Now, what ailed them all? It couldn't have been the advent of the Mayos. I've launched more ticklish craft than they. Nor could it have been that abominable Brian Beck, who would spoil Paradise and be the utter ruin of a respectable funeral. Every one seemed to conspire to make my dinner a failure."

"Oh, Sallie, I think Percival especially exerted himself. He was in his most exquisite mood."

"Oh, Percival, of course. He must have suspected that something was going wrong. Did you ever notice, when he talks, how Rachel turns her head away? But you can see the color creep up into her face. She is too proud and shy to let people see how much she cares for him. But when *she* speaks Percival looks at her with all his eyes, and positively leans forward so that he shall not miss a word. I love to watch those two. Sometimes when I have been with them I feel as if I had been to church."

Lilian Bell

"Then, too, Payson's manner to Nellie Mayo was the most chivalric thing I ever saw. He treated her as if the best in the land were not too good for her."

"Nor is it," said Sallie warmly.

"I'm glad you think so. What a sweet, unworldly spirit she has! Almost any woman would have been distressed because of her gown; but she was so superior to her dress, with that uplifted face of hers, that I felt ashamed to think of it myself. You gave her a rare pleasure last night, for she never meets clever men and women. The Percivals and Mr. Whitehouse delighted her, and you saw how well she sustained her part of the conversation. You see she thinks, if she doesn't have time to study. She was particularly fortunate in having Payson to take her out, for he has a faculty of putting people at their ease. Do you know, Sallie, Payson Osborne has come out wonderfully since you married him. He is more thoughtful, more considerate, and his manners always have been *so* good. I declare, last night I caught him looking at you in a way which made me quite fond of him."

"I'm fond of him myself," said Sallie candidly. "He undoubtedly is a dear old thing, and he is tremendously good to me. By the way, did you notice how red Frankie Taliaferro's eyes were last night? She had the toothache, poor girl. It came on quite suddenly just before dinner, and it alarmed me for fear she couldn't appear. Just before dinner I was naming over the way the people were to go in, and I said that I had to put engaged people together and separate husbands and wives, after the manner of real life, and Payson asked if I was sure Louise King and Charlie Hardy were engaged, and I said yes, although it never had been announced, and just then Frankie burst into tears. It was a suspicious time for crying, especially as that egregious flirt had paid her a great deal of attention; but Frankie would tell *me*, I am sure, and then she really had been to the dentist's that morning. So I gave her something for it which she said cured it. I was so vexed at her for making her eyes red, for her blue dress brought it out. If she had been crying over the other, she might have spared her tears, for I don't believe Charlie and Louise are engaged. I think they have quarrelled, for when Charlie offered his arm to Louise, she looked up with that way she has of throwing her head back, and I declare to you, Ruth, I saw, I positively saw, forked lightnings shoot from her eyes. They blazed so I was afraid they would set his tie on fire. As for Charlie, he turned first green, then magenta, then a rich and lively purple. I give you my word they did not speak to each other during that dinner, nor would Louise stay to the cotillon. Charlie danced it with Frankie. Nice state of affairs, isn't it?"

I felt myself grow weak. But Sallie proceeded gayly: "Then you know how hard I have tried to propitiate those miserable Asburys. I declare, I think Alice might meet me half way. Perhaps she didn't like being seated between Frank Mayo and Brian Beck, but both she and that awful Frost man sat as stiff and unsmiling as if they had swallowed curtain-poles by the dozen." Sallie does not mind an extra word or two to strengthen a simile. I tried to imagine Alice and Mr. Frost gulping down the articles Sallie mentioned, but mine was no match for Sallie's nimble fancy and I gave it up. "I do hope that Pet Winterbotham will not marry that man. I should as soon see her led to the altar by a satin-lined casket. I had to invite him when I found that Frankie could come. Wasn't Brian Beck dreadful, and didn't you think you would go to sleep under Frank Mayo's stories? And didn't Grace Beck's airs with Mr. Whitehouse amuse you? Oh, she will hold that head of hers so high if Pet marries Jack. How bored Asbury looked, didn't he? So selfish of him not to pretend to be pleased. Even Rachel vexed me by not being nicer to Asbury. I declare, Ruth, I was so irritated at the queer way every one acted, I felt as if it would be a relief to make faces at them, instead of beaming on them the hospitable beam of a hostess. I wonder how they would have liked it."

"They might have considered it rather unconventional perhaps."

Sallie smiled absent-mindedly, pressed her hand to her flushed cheek, looked over towards the Mayo house, and then, meeting my inquiring glance, dropped her eyes in confusion.

"Well," I said tentatively.

Sallie leaned back in her chair, put her hands behind her head, and closed her eyes.

"I wonder," she said dreamily, "why I ever attempt to do things. Why can't people let me alone, and why don't I let them alone? Most of all, why do I ever try to keep a secret?"

I knew then that she had been rattling on because her mind was full of something else. I don't believe she knew half that she had said. Presently to my surprise I saw a tear steal down her cheek.

"O Sallie!" I exclaimed, now really worried, "what is it?"

"I'll tell you, Ruth, for you are the only one who seems really to know and love that dear little Nellie Mayo and those blessed babies. Ruth, there is a Damocles sword hanging over that nest of birds, and it is liable to fall at any moment. Oh, it has weighed on my heart like lead ever since I discovered the secret. I know you don't like Frank Mayo, but you will despise him when I tell you the mischief he is up to, and that poor little wife of his trusting him as if he were an archangel. Oh, he is common, Ruth, and horrid, and if it is ever found out it will kill Nellie. But he is carrying on dreadfully with a soubrette in New York. He is wasting his money on her—and you know he has none to spare—and seems to be infatuated with her; while she, of course, is only using him to advertise herself. In fact, that is how I found it out. Payson is in a syndicate which is trying to buy one of those up-town theatres in New York and turn it into something else; I forget just what they want to do with it, but any way, he came in contact with the manager of the theatre where this woman was playing. He gave them a dinner and afterwards they occupied his box, and while this woman was on the stage her manager told how some man was causing nightly sensations by the flowers he sent her, and he said that he—her manager—thought he would have it written up for the papers to advertise her before she started out on her tour. He said the man was making a fool of himself, but the actress didn't care, and when he pointed out the fellow to them, Payson saw to his horror that it was Frank Mayo. He didn't say a word before the other gentlemen, but the next day he went to the manager and begged him to advertise the woman in some other way. He told him who Frank was and all about his poor little wife and the children, and the manager, who seems to be a good hearted man, said it was a shame and promised not to allow it. He even went so far as to offer to speak to the actress herself and request her to refuse to be interviewed on the subject. So Payson came home quite relieved. But the next time he saw the manager Payson asked him how things were going, and he said worse than ever as far as Frank himself was concerned, and he added that when he mentioned the subject to the actress she tossed her head and said Mayo must take care of himself.

"Then I thought I would do what I could to introduce him into society here, for you know he is ambitious in that line, and perhaps I might get him away from the creature. So I gave that whole thing yesterday for the Mayo family, with what result you know, except that I haven't told you that the presumptuous dolt made love mawkishly to me all the evening. Yes, actually! Did you ever hear of such impertinence? Oh, the man is simply insufferable, Ruth.

"Now, what I am constantly afraid of is that it will get into the papers after all. I read them, I fairly study them, so that it shall not escape me; but, if it does come out, what shall we do for Nellie? It will break her heart."

I looked at Sallie with gnawing conscience that I had ever called her lawn fete the climax of frivolity. The dear little soul! who would have suspected that she had such a worthy motive for her ball? But, do you know, sometimes in fashionable life we catch a glimpse of the simple-minded, homely kindliness which we are taught to believe exists only among horny-handed farmers, rough miners, and hardy mountaineers.

"Sallie, dear child," I said, "I beg your pardon for not knowing how noble you are."

"Noble? I? Sallie Cox? Now, nobody except Payson ever hinted at such a thing, and I hushed him up instantly. No, Ruth, it was nothing. I dare say Rachel or you would have thought of some grand project which would have been effectual, but *I* couldn't think of anything to do but to tickle his vanity by making him the guest of honor at the best affair of the season."

"Indeed, I think neither Rachel nor I could have thought of anything so sure to captivate a shallow mortal like Frank Mayo."

"Set a thief to catch a thief," said Sallie merrily. "I'm shallow myself, *I* knew how it would feel to have such a fine thing given for me. My dear, if the ball were only fine enough it would cure a broken heart."

"Not if the heart were really broken, Sallie."

"Well, you must admit that it would help *some*," she said whimsically.

And so she went away and left the burden upon me. Then I, too, fell to devouring the papers, as I knew Sallie was doing with me. I went more than ever to the little brown house which lay in such peril, and I never saw Nellie with a paper in her hand that I did not shudder.

At last the thing we so dreaded came to pass. In the evening paper there was quite a sensational account of it. Thank Heaven, no name was given; but alas, the description of him, of his wife and five little children, was unmistakable. I felt as though I had sat still and watched a cat kill a bird. It was raining, not hard, but drearily, and the dead leaves fluttered against the windows as the chill wind blew them from where they clung. I was lonesome, and the autumn evening intensified my feelings. I glanced over to where a red glow came from Nellie's windows. I fancied her sitting there with the paper in her hand, as she always did in the one spare moment of her busy day, with her heart crushed by the news. She would be alone, too, for Frank was out of town. Poor child! Poor child! I started up and decided to go and see her. If she didn't want me I could come back, but what if she did want me and I was not there?

I found her sitting, as I had expected, alone. The paper, with the fatal page uppermost, lay in her lap, as if she had read it and laid it down. There was only the firelight in the room.

Lilian Bell

"Come in, dear," she said gladly. "I was just thinking of you and wondering if such weather did not make you blue. Sit down here by the fire. It was sweet of you to come in the rain."

She searched my distressed face anxiously as she spoke. I made no reply. My heart was too full at being comforted when I had come to comfort. As I sat on a low stool at her side she seemed to divine my mood, for she drew my head against her knee with a mother touch, and threaded my hair with a mother hand, and pressed down my eyelids as I have seen her do when she puts her baby to sleep. And though she must have felt the tears come, she did not appear to know.

"Dear Ruth," she said, "I have been sitting here thinking about you, and wondering if you were satisfied, such a loving heart as you have, to face the rest of your life without the love you deserve. You won't be vexed with me for speaking of it to you, for you know I am so old-fashioned that I think love is the only thing in this world worth having. It is all that I live for. Of course my children love me, but, until they grow older, theirs is only an instinctive love. It isn't like the love of a husband, which singles you out of all the other countless women in the world to be his and only his forever. There is power enough in that thought to nerve the weakest woman to do a giant's task. The mere fact that you are all in all, the *only* woman, to the man you so dearly love, the one person who can make his world; when you think that your being away from one meal or out of the house when he comes in will make him miss you till his heart aches—this will keep down a moan of pain when it is almost beyond bearing, for fear it might cause him to suffer with you; it will nerve you to stand up and smile into his eyes when you are ready to drop with exhaustion. Love, such as a husband's love for his wife, is the most precious, the most supporting thing a woman can have. You never hear me talk much about my husband, but he is all this and more to me. I cannot begin to tell you about it. I read about unhappy marriages—why, I read a dreadful thing to-night in the paper, which set me to thinking how safe and happy I am, and how thankful I ought to be that I can trust my husband so. It was about a man who was unfaithful to his wife, and they had five children just as we have. I know such things do occur, but how or why is a mystery to me. I hope I am not too hard when I say that in such a case it must be the wife's fault. Surely if she had been a good wife, an unselfish and loving wife, he could not have been enticed away. Poor thing! I wonder how she felt when she heard it. Probably she wouldn't believe it. Probably she had too much faith in him. You shake your head. Why, Ruth, you dear thing, you don't know anything about it. A wife *couldn't* believe such a thing. Why, I wouldn't believe it if told by an angel from heaven. But then my husband is so dear to me. I do sometimes wonder if all women care as much for their husbands as I do for mine. Do you know, dear, I think about you so much. I know that there have been several hearts in which you have reigned, and yet you have not cared. But the true love, the right lover, has not come, or you could not have passed him by. He is waiting for you; somewhere, somehow, he will come to you, I am sure, and you will know then that you have belonged to each other all this time; that this love has been coming down the ages from eternity for just you two. You will not refuse it then. Why, I could never have refused to marry Frank when I found that I was as much to him as he was to me! He is so handsome, so good. I shall never cease to thank God that He made him turn aside into the quiet places to find me. But, in spite of all this, you know I don't think he is perfect. He doesn't care for books as much as I wish he did. He has no ear for music, and he cannot tell a story straight to save his life, the dear boy! Love does not blind my eyes, but this is what it does do. It makes me overlook in him what would annoy me in others. When, at that beautiful dinner of Mrs. Osborne's, Frank told

Lilian Bell

those stories of his that I've heard for years, I don't think any one cared to hear them except Mr. Beck and me. I knew they were not well told, but it was my husband who was telling them, and I could listen to his voice, even if I couldn't sit next him.

"How the wind blows. Don't you think it has a lonesome sound to-night? There isn't a glimmer of light from any of your windows yet, and see what a lovely glow this fire casts all through the room. It makes the cold walls look warm, and if it makes shadows, it chases them away when it blazes its brightest. It is your fault that there is no light in your windows, and your fault that you have closed your heart against love. You could have the glow that lights my house and my heart if you only would. You know, dear, I am not talking to you as a neighbor now or even as a friend, but as a woman talks to a woman out of her inmost heart. It is only because I love you so and because I have seen you with my babies that I know what a home-maker you are. You seem so sad sometimes, and I know your heart is wistful if your eyes are not. How can you have the courage to shut out love? How can you see the happiness of all your friends and not want a share of it yourself? Why do you cry so, my dear? Is there some one you love? Has any trouble come between you? No? No? Well, there, there! It was selfish of me to show you the way I look at things and to try to make you dissatisfied. Never mind. You are stronger than I. I could not live without love; I should die. But if you can, it may be that you are fulfilling your destiny more nobly than many another who has more of what I should choose.

"Oh, must you go? Forgive me if I have said what I should not. Good-night, and God bless you, my dear."

XI

THE HAZARD OF A HUMAN DIE

"The tallest trees are most in the power of the wind."

Last night at the theatre there were theatricals all over the house. My eyes followed the play on the stage, but my mind was filled with the farce in the next box and with the tragedy in the one opposite.

I was with the Ford-Burkes, and, hearing familiar voices, I pulled aside the curtain, and in the next box were the Payson Osbornes, Pet Winterbotham, and Jack Whitehouse. Pet thrust her hand over the railing and whispered,

"I'm engaged. Put your hand here and feel the size of my ring. You can get an idea of it through my glove. I'd take it off and show it to you, only I think it would look rather pronounced, don't you?"

"Rather," I assented faintly.

I glanced beyond her into the fresh blue eyes of young Jack Whitehouse, and I wondered if the alert, manly young fellow, with his untried but inherited capabilities, knew that he had been accepted as a husband because his hair curled and he looked "chappie."

"I suppose you have heard the news, haven't you?" she went on.

"Nothing in particular. What news?"

"Look across the house and you will see."

Just entering their box opposite were Louise King and Norris Whitehouse, Jack's uncle.

"What do you mean?" I asked, with a wrench at Pet's little hand which made her wince.

"It's an engagement. Uncle and nephew engaged the same season. Isn't it rich? Think of Louise King being my aunt. She is only twenty-three."

Then they saw us and bowed. I felt faint as my mind adjusted itself to this new arrangement. I levelled my glass at them.

Louise, magnificently tall and handsome, looked quite self-contained. She is one of the best-bred girls I know, but it required a stronger imagination than mine to fathom what mysterious change had transformed her from the impulsive, loving creature of Charlie Hardy's story to this serene-eyed woman, who had deliberately elected to marry at the funeral of her own heart.

As I looked across at her during that long evening, I felt that it was impertinent to probe her heart with my wonderings and surmises. I knew instinctively just how carefully she was hiding her hurt from all human eyes. I knew how her fierce pride was bearing up under the cruelty of it. I felt how she had rushed from the humiliation one man had brought her to the waiting love of the one who should have been her first choice by the divine right of natural selection. This strong man had loved her for years, but he would never allow her to imperil either his dignity or her own. He was just the man her impulsive, high-strung nature could accept as a refuge, beat against and buffet if need be, then learn to appreciate and cling to.

I had an impression that he was not totally ignorant of the state of affairs. He was older and wiser than she, and capable of the bravery of this venture. No, he was not being deceived. I was sure of it. Louise was too high minded to attempt it. She would be scornfully honest with him. Her scorn would be for herself, not for him, and he had accepted her joyfully on these terms. His daring was tempered with prudence, and his clear vision doubtless forecast the end. His insight must have shown him that, with a girl like Louise, the rebound from the self-disdain to which Charlie Hardy's confession must have reduced her would be as intense as her humiliation had been, and that her passionate gratitude to the man who restored her self-respect would be boundless. Not every man—not even every man who loved her—could do this. He must possess strong nerves who descends into a volcano. He must have a more unbending will who tames any wild thing; but what an intoxicating thrill of pride must come to him who, having confidence in his own powers, makes the attempt and succeeds.

Perhaps if Louise had been strong enough to fight this cruel battle out with herself as Rachel would have done, and win as Rachel would have won, she might have been able to choose differently. She might then, strong in her own strength, marry a man of lesser personality, a younger man, and they two could have adjusted their lives to each other gradually. Now it must be Louise who would be adjusted, and Norris Whitehouse was just the man to know the curious fact that the more fiery and impetuous a woman is, the more easily, if she is in love, will she mould herself to circumstances. The more untamed and unbending she seems, the more helpless will she be under the strong excitement of love or grief.

A strong-minded woman is easier to persuade than a weak one. The grander the nature the greater its pliability towards truth. The longer I sat and gazed into the opposite box the clearer it grew in my mind that the suddenness of this venture did not imply rashness, but serene-eyed faith only, and such faith would captivate Louise King more than would love. The only impossible thing about it to a sceptical Old Maid was that it was the man who was proving himself such a hero, and who was upsetting my favorite theory that men never understand emotional women. Still, it was not difficult to except as unusual a man like Norris Whitehouse, and yet have my theory hold good. In imagination I leaped forward to the peaceful outcome of this turbulent beginning, and overlooked the way which led to it. I found myself hoping, with painful intensity, that this venture in which Norris Whitehouse and I had embarked would prove successful. I had known and loved Louise King all her life. I had loved her dear mother before her, and the beautiful daughterhood of this girl had always touched me as the highest and sweetest type I ever had known. I did not want to be the one to bring her face to face with her first great sorrow, although I dared not interfere to less purpose. For

> "'Tis an awkward thing to play with souls,
> And matter enough to save one's own.
> Yet think of my friend and the burning coals
> We played with for bits of stone."

They could not know that I had had anything to do with it;

yet, if ill came of it, I should blame myself all the rest of my life.

Not long afterwards they were married very quietly and went away for a few weeks. When they returned I sought Louise with eagerness, and found that my fears were not groundless. I tried to think what to do. If it would have eased matters, I would willingly have gone to her and confessed that I instigated Charlie Hardy's confession. But I felt that the root of the matter lay deeper than that, so I said nothing that could be construed into an unwelcome knowledge of her affairs.

In the short time which elapsed between their return and the date set for their departure for Europe, where they were to stay a year, I saw Louise continually. She sought me as if she liked to be with me, although her eyes never lost the anxious, hunted expression which you sometimes see in the eyes of some trapped wild creature.

It was a raw morning, with a chill wind blowing, when their steamer was to sail. Mr. Whitehouse, thinking I might have some last private word to say to Louise, skilfully detached everybody else and strolled with them beyond earshot, but where his eyes could continually rest upon his wife's face.

As Louise and I walked up and down I took in mine the small hand which emerged from the great fur cuff of her boat cloak, and gradually its rigidity relaxed under my friendly pressure. I remembered, as I occasionally tightened my grasp upon it, that my dear little baby sister Lois, who was taken away from us before she outgrew her babyhood, used to squeeze my hand in this fashion, and when I asked her what it meant, she invariably said, "It means dat it loves you." I wondered if the same inarticulate language could be conveyed to poor, suffering Louise. Suddenly she turned to me and said,

"You have thrown something gentle, a softness around me this morning. I can feel it. What is it, Ruth?"

"I don't know, dear, unless it is my love for you."

"It is something more. Your eyes look into mine as if you knew all about it and wished to comfort me."

As I made no answer, she turned and looked down at me from her superb height.

"Tell me," she said quite gently; "I shall not be angry. Tell me, *do* you know?"

"Yes, Louise, I know."

She hesitated a moment as if she really had not believed it. Then she said slowly,

"If any other person on earth except you had told me that, I should die. I could not live in the knowledge. But you—well, your pity is not an insult somehow."

"Because it is not pity, Louise," I said steadily. "There is a difference between pity and sympathy. One is thrown at you—the other walks with you."

She only pressed my hand gratefully. Suddenly she turned and said impulsively,

"Then you must know how utterly wretched I am."

Glancing over her shoulder I could see the eyes of her husband fastened upon her with an expression which stirred me to put forth my best efforts.

Then it came over me how pent-up all this intensity of feeling must be. I realized how impossible it would seem to her to speak of it. Taking my life in my hand—for I was mortally afraid—I rushed in, after the manner of my kind, where angels fear to tread.

"Did you love him then so much?"

The pupils of her eyes enlarged until they were all black with excitement. She caught both my hands in hers.

"Only God Himself knows how I loved him," she whispered.

I knew then that all Charlie had said was true, and, weak coward that I was, if I could have undone the past, I would have given him back to her. I was borne away by a glimpse of such love. O Charlie Hardy! And you cast this from you for a pair of blue eyes!

"How came you to love such a weak man?" I asked tremblingly.

"That is what I want to know. How could I? How can girls of my sort love so hopelessly beneath us? I've thought and wondered over that question until my brain has almost turned, and the only consolation I find is that I am not the only one. Other women, cleverer than I, have loved the most contemptible of men and have been deceived just as I was. Oh, if he or I had only died before I discovered the truth! If I could have mourned him honorably and felt that my grief was dignified! But I won't allow myself to grieve over him. I tell myself that I am well out of it and that I ought to be glad. But instead of gladness there is a dull, miserable ache in my heart, which I feel even in my sleep. Not for him; I don't mourn for him, but for myself—for my fallen idols and my shattered ideals. What will such men have to answer for? I doubt if I ever can believe in anything human again."

"Anything *human*," I repeated gladly.

Louise looked down.

"He was not omnipotent," she said huskily. "He ruled my heart only, not my soul."

"I suppose you have tried to love your husband?" I said.

"Tried? Oh, Ruth, I have tried so hard! He is so good to me. He knows everything. Of course I told him. That was why we were married so suddenly. He wished it and urged such excellent reasons, and I had so much respect for him and his wisdom in what is best, that I married him. I thought I could love him. I always thought that if I didn't love—the other one—I should love Norris; but I can't. I believe my power of love is gone forever. I feel sometimes as if the best part of me had been killed—not died of its own accord, but as if it had been murdered."

"Poor child!" I said. "Why don't you talk this over with your husband?"

"Oh, Ruth, how could I?"

"Well, may I talk to you? Will it hurt you?"

"Nothing that you would say can hurt me, dear."

"Then let me say just this. You have been trying to do in weeks what nature would take years to do. In real life you cannot lose your love and heal your worse than widowed heart and love anew as you would in private theatricals. You have outraged your own delicate sensibilities, but not with your husband's consent. He does not want you to try to love him. No good man does. He wants you to love him because you can't help yourself—because it seems to your heart to be the only natural thing to do. 'When the song's gone out of your life, you can't start another while it's a-ringing in your ears. It's best to have a bit o' silence, and out of that maybe a psalm'll come by and by.'"

"Oh, Ruth, dear Ruth, say that again," she cried, turning towards me with tears in her lovely eyes. I repeated it.

"How restful to dare to take 'a bit o' silence'!"

"No one can prevent you doing so but yourself. Mr. Whitehouse married you to give you just that, confident that he loved you so much that the psalm would come by and by."

"I believe he did," said Louise gently, with color rising in her cheeks.

"Another thing. Don't try not to grieve. Don't repress yourself. It is right that you should mourn over your lost ideals. Nothing on earth brings more poignant grief than that. You will never get them back. Do not expect what is impossible. They were false ideals, none the less beautiful and dear to you for being that, but truly they were distorted. You will see this some time. You have begun to see it now. You realize that this man was in no way what you thought him. You had idealized him, had almost crowned him. Now you can't help trying to invest Mr. Whitehouse with the same unnamable, invisible qualities. But no man has them. Your husband is a thousand times more worthy than the other, yet even he does not deserve worship. Let the man do the crowning if you can, although a woman of your temperament would find even that difficult—that which the most inane of women could accept with calmness and a smile. You have the magnificent humility of the truly great. Still it is not appreciated in this world. Try resting for a while and let your husband love you."

I knew that I was saying, though perhaps in a different way, things which Norris Whitehouse had urged upon her. Not that she said so. She would have regarded that as sacrilege. But it was a look, a little trembling smile, which betrayed the ingenuous young creature to me. I felt that I was in the presence of a nature very fair and exquisitely pure. It was a sacred feeling. I almost felt as if I ought not to read the signs in her face, because she had no idea that they were there.

"I have such horrible doubts," she said suddenly with suppressed bitterness. "I do not belittle my love. I know that I loved him with all my heart and soul, and that I gave him more than most women would have done, because love means infinitely more to me than it does to them. I knew all the time that I loved him more than he loved me, but I did not care, for I believed, blind as I was, that we loved each other all we were capable of doing, and if I had more love to give it was only because I was richer than he, and I meant to make him the greater by my treasure. Now I feel that both I and my love have been wasted. Oh, it was a cruel thing, Ruth. I feel so poor, so poor."

"Louise, you think, but you do not think rightly. *Are* you poorer for having loved him? What is his unworth compared with your worth? Isn't your love sweeter and truer for having grown and expanded? No love was ever wasted. It enriches the giver involuntarily. You are a sweeter, better woman than before you loved, unless you made the mistake of small natures and let it embitter you. You have no right to feel that it has been wasted."

"Do you think so?" she said doubtfully. "That is an uplifting thought." Then she added in a low voice, "There is one thing more. It is very unworthy, I am afraid, but it is a canker that is eating my heart out. And that is the mortification of it. Can you picture the thing to yourself? Can you form any idea of how I felt? It grows worse the more I think of it."

"I know, I know. But, dear child, there is where I am powerless to help you. If I were in your place I think I should feel just as you do. It was a cruel thing. I wonder that you bore it as well as you did."

"What! Should *you* feel that way? Then you do not blame me?"

"Why mention blame in connection with yourself? You are singularly free from it. But did you ever consider what an honor the love of such a man as your husband is? Do you know how he is admired by great men? Do you realize how he must love you, and what magnificent faith he must have to wish to marry a young girl like you who admits that she does not love him? If you never do anything else in this world except to deserve the faith he has in you, you will live a worthy life."

We were standing still now, and Louise was looking at her husband at a distance with a look in her eyes which was good to see.

"You never can love him as you loved the other one. A first love never comes again. Would you want it to? When you love your husband, as he and I both know that you will do some time—perhaps not soon, but he is very patient—still, I say, when you love him you will love him in a gentler, truer way."

"Can you tell me why such a bitter experience should have been sent to me so early in life?"

"To save you pain later and to make of you what you were planned to be."

Tears rolled down her cheeks and she bent to kiss me, for the last mail had been put aboard and we had only a moment more.

What she whispered in my ear I shall never tell to any one, but it will sweeten my whole life.

As we went towards Mr. Whitehouse Louise involuntarily quickened her pace a little and held out her hand to him with a smile. It was good to see his face change color and to view the quiet delight with which he received her.

Then there were good-byes and hurried steps and a great deal of shouting and hauling of ropes, and there were waving of hands and a tossing of roses from the decks above and a few furtive tears and many heart-aches, and then—the great steamer had sailed.

XII

IN WHICH I WILLINGLY
TURN MY FACE WESTWARD

"Grow old along with me.
The best is yet to be,
The last of life, for which the first was made.
Our times are in His hand
Who saith, 'A whole I planned,
Youth shows but half; trust God, see all, nor be afraid.'"

The years cannot go on without destroying the old land-marks, and I am so old-fashioned that change of any kind saddens me. People move away, strangers take their houses, the girls marry, children grow up, and everything is so mutable that sometimes my cheerfulness has a haze to it.

I am in a mood of retrospection to-night. I am living over the past and knitting up the ravelled ends.

Dear Rachel! I am thankful that she and Percival continue so happy. It is wonderful how every one recognizes and speaks of the completeness of these two. They do not parade their affection. They seem rather to try to hide it even from me, as if it were almost too sacred for even my kindly eyes. It is in the atmosphere, and, though they go their separate ways, they are more thoroughly together than any other married people I know.

Both Percival and Rachel are becoming very generally recognized now. People are discovering how wonderfully clever their work is, and they share themselves with the public, although it is a sacrifice every time they do so. Rachel's rather turbulent cleverness has softened down. She says it is because it is "billowed in another greater and gentler sort." She looks at me rather wistfully sometimes. I know what she thinks, but she does not bore me with questions. I wonder if she thinks I regret anything. Unless I consider that the Percivals have redeemed the record I am keeping, there is nothing especially tempting in the marriages I am watching. I cannot think that they are any happier than I am.

Sallie Cox seems contented most of the time. She has a magnificent establishment, handsomer than all the rest of the girls' put together. Her husband "doesn't bother" her, she says, and the Osbornes are very popular.

"I'm glad I'm shallow," she said to me once. "Shallow hearts do not ache long. If I had a deep nature I should go mad or turn into a saint. As it is, I wear the scars."

Once, when I went with her to Rachel's, she sat and looked around the simple, inexpensive house, with the walls all lined with books and no room too good to live in every day, and she said,

"This is the prettiest home I ever was in in my life, and there is not a lace curtain in the house!"

We laughed—everybody laughs at Sallie—and Rachel

said gently,

"We don't need them."

Sallie looked up quickly and took in the full significance of the words, as she answered in the same tone,

"No, you do not, but I do." And each woman had told her heart history. Now, Rachel must know almost as much about Sallie as I do; but she never will know all.

Sallie said she went home and hated every room in her house separately and specifically; then she had a good cry over "the perfectness of the Percivals," and issued invitations to a masked ball.

"That ball was full of significance, Ruth," she told me afterwards with her most whimsically knowing look. "It was bristling with it. But nobody thought of it except a certain little goose I know named Sara Cox Osborne."

Jack Whitehouse and Pet Winterbotham are married. They had the most beautiful wedding I ever saw; but it was like watching the babes in the wood, for they are *such* a young-looking pair.

I understand better now what Pet meant when she talked about Jack's appearance so much. I think he expressed to her the idea of perpetual youth and eternal spring-time. To me, too, it seems as if he ought always to be yachting in blue and white, or lying at full length on the grass at some girl's feet. And Pet herself makes an admirable companion-piece. When I see her in a misty white ball-dress, with one man bringing her an ice and another holding her flowers and a third bearing her filmy wraps, I feel that things are quite as they should be. Some people seem to be born for fair weather and smooth sailing.

It is too soon to judge them finally. Norris Whitehouse's nephew will outgrow the ball-room, and Pet will find in Louise an incentive to grow womanly.

The Asburys have built a fine house since Alice's father died, and go about a great deal, but seldom together. Asbury lives at the club, and Alice has her mother with her. Alice has embraced Theosophy and spells her name "Alys." She always is interested in something new and advanced, and whenever I meet her I am prepared to go into ecstasies over a plan to save men's souls by electricity, or something equally speedy in the moral line. She is daft on spiritual rapid transit.

She does these things because she is a disappointed, clever, ambitious woman, who would have made a noble character if she had been surrounded by right influences.

What would have been the result if Alice had taken as her creed: "The situation that has not its duty, its ideals, was never yet occupied by man. Yes, here in this poor, miserable, hampered, despicable Actual, wherein thou even now standest, here or nowhere is thy Ideal; work it out therefrom, and working, live, be free. Fool! the Ideal is in thyself; thy condition is but the stuff thou art to shape that same ideal out of; what matters whether such stuff be of this sort or that, so the form thou give it be heroic, be poetic? Oh, thou that pinest in the imprisonment of the Actual and criest bitterly to the gods for a kingdom wherein to rule and create, know this of a truth: the thing thou seekest is already with thee, 'here or nowhere,' couldst thou only see"?

Ah, well, she could not. She still is crying to the gods and spelling her name "Alys." Her cleverness must have an outlet, and, with worse than no husband to lavish it upon, she scatters it to the four winds of heaven and gets herself talked about as "queer."

May Brandt has bitten into her apples of Sodom, and the taste of ashes is bitter indeed to her. She knows now that Brandt never loved her, and did love Alice. I do not know whether she thinks he still cares for Alice or not. May never had much beauty to lose, but she looks worn and unhappy, and watches Alice with a degree of feeling which would appear vulgar to me if I did not know just how miserable she is. She is hopelessly plain now, and Alice is still like a tall, stately lily. Brandt devours her with his eyes, but Alice makes him keep his distance.

Sallie Cox has been diplomatic and harmless enough to make Alice forgive her, and they are quite good friends; but Alice is magnificent in her scorn of Brandt's wife, who almost cowers in her presence.

Poor May! I wish I could take that look of suffering from her little pinched, three-cornered face for just one hour. But how could I? How could anybody who knew all about it?

She does not understand Alice in all her moods and vagaries, and Alice does not condescend to explain herself even to her friends. I do not believe that Alice and Brandt have ever spoken on the subject which occupies three minds whenever they two are thrown together. Yet I imagine it would be a relief to May if she were told that. However, she is scarcely noble enough to believe it, even if Alice herself should tell her. But Alice never will. She never gives it a thought. Brandt, too, has honor, though, even if he had not, Alice would have it for him and forbid a word.

It is a fortunate thing for some people's chances for a future life that there are a reasonable number of consciences distributed through the world, although it would be an Old Maid's suggestion that sometimes they be allowed to drive instead of being used as a liveried tiger—for ornament and always behind. It is a great pity that people who are supplied with them—and well-cultivated consciences too—have not the courage to live up to them, but allow themselves to be gently and feebly miserable all their lives.

Now, Charlie Hardy has periods of being the most miserable man I ever knew. His last interview with Louise must have been as serious a thing as he ever experienced. He has married Frankie Taliaferro, and she makes the sweetest little kitten of a wife you ever saw. In Louise he would have been protected by a coat of mail. In Frankie he finds it turned into a pale-blue eider-down quilt, which suits his temperament much better.

Louise Whitehouse is coming home soon. Her year abroad has lengthened into several years, and they have been the most beautiful of her life, she writes. "Living with a song in one's life may be the sweetest while it lasts and before one thinks; but to live by a psalm is to find life infinitely more beautiful and worthier. I never can be thankful enough that my life was taken out of my hands at the time when I clung to it most blindly, and ordered anew by One stronger and wiser than I."

Tears come to my eyes whenever I think of this girl. I do not quite know why, unless it is that there always is something sad in watching the tempering of a bright young enthusiasm, even though it becomes more useful than when so sparkling and high-strung.

I have been at great pains to have Charlie Hardy realize how happy Louise is, but his conscience still troubles him at times. He says he knows he did the right thing for every one concerned, but he dislikes the idea of himself in so disagreeable a role; and Louise's opinion of him now, after the one she did have, is a constant humiliation to him. Women always have admired him, and he objects very strongly to any exception to the rule. I think he misses the mental ozone which he found in Louise. I often wonder if men who have loved superior women and married average ones do not have occasional wonderings and yearnings over lost "might have beens."

The Mayos still live in the brown house, which has been enlarged and greatly beautified recently. I have an enthusiastic friendship with the children, who are growing into slim slips of girls and sturdy, clear-eyed boys, and their house is still a home. Frank's admiration for soubrettes died a sudden and violent death at the masked notoriety of his initial escapade, and for a time he was shocked into better behavior. We hear odd rumors floating around, however, of whose truth we never can be sure, but which we shake our heads over, after the fashion of those whose confidence has been caught napping once. We never knew whether Nellie discovered the truth or not. If Frank denied it, it would not affect matters with her if the world rang with it. Her idolatry has a certain blind stubbornness in it which I should not care to beat against.

Bronson does not stand as straight as he did when I first knew him. Rachel says he has "a scholarly stoop." But she knows, and I know, that something besides law-books and parchment has taken the elasticity out of his step.

Many years have gone by since I became an Old Maid. I want to call my Alter Ego's attention to this fact gently but firmly, because I have an idea that she still considers herself "only thirty," and that she thinks she has just begun to be an Old Maid. Whereas she is old and so am I. I do not mind it at all. Neither does she; it is only that she had not realized it. We have so much to think about more important than our stupid ages. People have grown used to seeing us about, and we like the same things, and keep going at about the same pace and in the same road, and I think we have come to be an Institution.

I have no worries which I do not borrow from my married friends. I keep up with the fashions; my clothes fit me; my fingers still come to the ends of my gloves; I feel no leaning towards all-over cloth shoes; I have not gone permanently into bonnets. I have tried to be a pleasant Old Maid, and my reward is that my friends make me feel as if they liked to have me about. I am not made to feel that I am *passe*. One's clothes and one's feelings are all that ever make one *passe*.

Nevertheless, I have turned my face resolutely towards the setting sun. I am resting now. I have given up struggling against the inevitable. That is a privilege and an attribute of youth. I feel as though I were only beginning to live, now that I have passed through the period of turmoil and come out from the rapids into gently gliding water. There is so much in life which we could not see at the beginning, but which grows with our growth and bears us company in the richness of evening-tide. I have learned to love my life and to cultivate it. Who knows what is in her life until she has tended it and made it know that she expects something from it in return for all her aspirations and endeavors? Even my wasted efforts are dear to me.

> "'Tis greatly wise to talk with our past hours,
> And ask them what report they bore to Heaven,
> And how they might have borne more welcome news."

Yet there is a sadness in looking back. I see the many lost opportunities lifting to me their wistful faces, and dumbly pleading with me to accept them and their promises; yet I carelessly passed them by. I see worse. I see the rents in the hedge, where I forced my wilful way into forbidden fields, and only regained my path after weary wandering, brier-torn, and none the better for my folly. Lost faces come before me which I might have gladdened oftener. Voices sound in my ear whose tones I might have made happier if I would. Withheld sympathy rises up before me deploring its wasted treasure. How can any one be happy in looking back? The only pleasure in looking forward is in hope. Yet now both grief and joy are tempered with a softness which enfolds my fretted spirit gratefully.

"Time has laid his hand
Upon my heart gently; not smiting it,
But as a harper lays his open palm
Upon his harp to deaden its vibrations."

And so I am looking forward to-night to an old age more peaceful, less turbulent, than my youth has been. I reach forward gladly, too, for life holds much that is sweet to old age, which youth can in no wise comprehend. Possibly this is one reason why youth is so anxious to concentrate enjoyment. But I am tired of concentration. There is a wear and tear about it which precludes the possibility of pleasure. I want to take the rest of my life gently, and by redoubled tenderness repay it for rude handling in my youth—that youth which lies very far away from me to-night and is wrapped in a rainbow mist.

THE END

Lilian Bell

Other books by this author

As Seen By Me
At Home with the Jardines
From A Girls Point Of View

Choose from Thousands of 1stWorldLibrary Classics By

A. M. Barnard
Ada Leverson
Adolphus William Ward
Aesop
Agatha Christie
Alexander Aaronsohn
Alexander Kielland
Alexandre Dumas
Alfred Gatty
Alfred Ollivant
Alice Duer Miller
Alice Turner Curtis
Alice Dunbar
Allen Chapman
Alleyne Ireland
Ambrose Bierce
Amelia E. Barr
Amory H. Bradford
Andrew Lang
Andrew McFarland Davis
Andy Adams
Angela Brazil
Anna Alice Chapin
Anna Sewell
Annie Besant
Annie Hamilton Donnell
Annie Payson Call
Annie Roe Carr
Annonaymous
Anton Chekhov
Archibald Lee Fletcher
Arnold Bennett
Arthur C. Benson
Arthur Conan Doyle
Arthur M. Winfield
Arthur Ransome
Arthur Schnitzler
Arthur Train
Atticus
B.H. Baden-Powell
B. M. Bower
B. C. Chatterjee
Baroness Emmuska Orczy
Baroness Orczy
Basil King
Bayard Taylor
Ben Macomber
Bertha Muzzy Bower
Bjornstjerne Bjornson

Booth Tarkington
Boyd Cable
Bram Stoker
C. Collodi
C. E. Orr
C. M. Ingleby
Carolyn Wells
Catherine Parr Traill
Charles A. Eastman
Charles Amory Beach
Charles Dickens
Charles Dudley Warner
Charles Farrar Browne
Charles Ives
Charles Kingsley
Charles Klein
Charles Hanson Towne
Charles Lathrop Pack
Charles Romyn Dake
Charles Whibley
Charles Willing Beale
Charlotte M. Braeme
Charlotte M. Yonge
Charlotte Perkins Stetson
Clair W. Hayes
Clarence Day Jr.
Clarence E. Mulford
Clemence Housman
Confucius
Coningsby Dawson
Cornelis DeWitt Wilcox
Cyril Burleigh
D. H. Lawrence
Daniel Defoe
David Garnett
Dinah Craik
Don Carlos Janes
Donald Keyhoe
Dorothy Kilner
Dougan Clark
Douglas Fairbanks
E. Nesbit
E. P. Roe
E. Phillips Oppenheim
E. S. Brooks
Earl Barnes
Edgar Rice Burroughs
Edith Van Dyne
Edith Wharton

Edward Everett Hale
Edward J. O'Biren
Edward S. Ellis
Edwin L. Arnold
Eleanor Atkins
Eleanor Hallowell Abbott
Eliot Gregory
Elizabeth Gaskell
Elizabeth McCracken
Elizabeth Von Arnim
Ellem Key
Emerson Hough
Emilie F. Carlen
Emily Bronte
Emily Dickinson
Enid Bagnold
Enilor Macartney Lane
Erasmus W. Jones
Ernie Howard Pie
Ethel May Dell
Ethel Turner
Ethel Watts Mumford
Eugene Sue
Eugenie Foa
Eugene Wood
Eustace Hale Ball
Evelyn Everett-green
Everard Cotes
F. H. Cheley
F. J. Cross
F. Marion Crawford
Fannie E. Newberry
Federick Austin Ogg
Ferdinand Ossendowski
Fergus Hume
Florence A. Kilpatrick
Fremont B. Deering
Francis Bacon
Francis Darwin
Frances Hodgson Burnett
Frances Parkinson Keyes
Frank Gee Patchin
Frank Harris
Frank Jewett Mather
Frank L. Packard
Frank V. Webster
Frederic Stewart Isham
Frederick Trevor Hill
Frederick Winslow Taylor

Friedrich Kerst
Friedrich Nietzsche
Fyodor Dostoyevsky
G.A. Henty
G.K. Chesterton
Gabrielle E. Jackson
Garrett P. Serviss
Gaston Leroux
George A. Warren
George Ade
Geroge Bernard Shaw
George Cary Eggleston
George Durston
George Ebers
George Eliot
George Gissing
George MacDonald
George Meredith
George Orwell
George Sylvester Viereck
George Tucker
George W. Cable
George Wharton James
Gertrude Atherton
Gordon Casserly
Grace E. King
Grace Gallatin
Grace Greenwood
Grant Allen
Guillermo A. Sherwell
Gulielma Zollinger
Gustav Flaubert
H. A. Cody
H. B. Irving
H. C. Bailey
H. G. Wells
H. H. Munro
H. Irving Hancock
H. R. Naylor
H. Rider Haggard
H. W. C. Davis
Haldeman Julius
Hall Caine
Hamilton Wright Mabie
Hans Christian Andersen
Harold Avery
Harold McGrath
Harriet Beecher Stowe
Harry Castlemon
Harry Coghill
Harry Houidini

Hayden Carruth
Helent Hunt Jackson
Helen Nicolay
Hendrik Conscience
Hendy David Thoreau
Henri Barbusse
Henrik Ibsen
Henry Adams
Henry Ford
Henry Frost
Henry James
Henry Jones Ford
Henry Seton Merriman
Henry W Longfellow
Herbert A. Giles
Herbert Carter
Herbert N. Casson
Herman Hesse
Hildegard G. Frey
Homer
Honore De Balzac
Horace B. Day
Horace Walpole
Horatio Alger Jr.
Howard Pyle
Howard R. Garis
Hugh Lofting
Hugh Walpole
Humphry Ward
Ian Maclaren
Inez Haynes Gillmore
Irving Bacheller
Isabel Cecilia Williams
Isabel Hornibrook
Israel Abrahams
Ivan Turgenev
J. G.Austin
J. Henri Fabre
J. M. Barrie
J. M. Walsh
J. Macdonald Oxley
J. R. Miller
J. S. Fletcher
J. S. Knowles
J. Storer Clouston
J. W. Duffield
Jack London
Jacob Abbott
James Allen
James Andrews
James Baldwin

James Branch Cabell
James DeMille
James Joyce
James Lane Allen
James Lane Allen
James Oliver Curwood
James Oppenheim
James Otis
James R. Driscoll
Jane Abbott
Jane Austen
Jane L. Stewart
Janet Aldridge
Jens Peter Jacobsen
Jerome K. Jerome
Jessie Graham Flower
John Buchan
John Burroughs
John Cournos
John F. Kennedy
John Gay
John Glasworthy
John Habberton
John Joy Bell
John Kendrick Bangs
John Milton
John Philip Sousa
John Taintor Foote
Jonas Lauritz Idemil Lie
Jonathan Swift
Joseph A. Altsheler
Joseph Carey
Joseph Conrad
Joseph E. Badger Jr
Joseph Hergesheimer
Joseph Jacobs
Jules Vernes
Julian Hawthrone
Julie A Lippmann
Justin Huntly McCarthy
Kakuzo Okakura
Karle Wilson Baker
Kate Chopin
Kenneth Grahame
Kenneth McGaffey
Kate Langley Bosher
Kate Langley Bosher
Katherine Cecil Thurston
Katherine Stokes
L. A. Abbot
L. T. Meade

L. Frank Baum	Owen Johnson	Stephen Crane
Latta Griswold	P.G. Wodehouse	Stewart Edward White
Laura Dent Crane	Paul and Mabel Thorne	Stijn Streuvels
Laura Lee Hope	Paul G. Tomlinson	Swami Abhedananda
Laurence Housman	Paul Severing	Swami Parmananda
Lawrence Beasley	Percy Brebner	T. S. Ackland
Leo Tolstoy	Percy Keese Fitzhugh	T. S. Arthur
Leonid Andreyev	Peter B. Kyne	The Princess Der Ling
Lewis Carroll	Plato	Thomas A. Janvier
Lewis Sperry Chafer	Quincy Allen	Thomas A Kempis
Lilian Bell	R. Derby Holmes	Thomas Anderton
Lloyd Osbourne	R. L. Stevenson	Thomas Bailey Aldrich
Louis Hughes	R. S. Ball	Thomas Bulfinch
Louis Joseph Vance	Rabindranath Tagore	Thomas De Quincey
Louis Tracy	Rahul Alvares	Thomas Dixon
Louisa May Alcott	Ralph Bonehill	Thomas H. Huxley
Lucy Fitch Perkins	Ralph Henry Barbour	Thomas Hardy
Lucy Maud Montgomery	Ralph Victor	Thomas More
Luther Benson	Ralph Waldo Emmerson	Thornton W. Burgess
Lydia Miller Middleton	Rene Descartes	U. S. Grant
Lyndon Orr	Ray Cummings	Upton Sinclair
M. Corvus	Rex Beach	Valentine Williams
M. H. Adams	Rex E. Beach	Various Authors
Margaret E. Sangster	Richard Harding Davis	Vaughan Kester
Margret Howth	Richard Jefferies	Victor Appleton
Margaret Vandercook	Richard Le Gallienne	Victor G. Durham
Margaret W. Hungerford	Robert Barr	Victoria Cross
Margret Penrose	Robert Frost	Virginia Woolf
Maria Edgeworth	Robert Gordon Anderson	Wadsworth Camp
Maria Thompson Daviess	Robert L. Drake	Walter Camp
Mariano Azuela	Robert Lansing	Walter Scott
Marion Polk Angellotti	Robert Lynd	Washington Irving
Mark Overton	Robert Michael Ballantyne	Wilbur Lawton
Mark Twain	Robert W. Chambers	Wilkie Collins
Mary Austin	Rosa Nouchette Carey	Willa Cather
Mary Catherine Crowley	Rudyard Kipling	Willard F. Baker
Mary Cole	Saint Augustine	William Dean Howells
Mary Hastings Bradley	Samuel B. Allison	William le Queux
Mary Roberts Rinehart	Samuel Hopkins Adams	W. Makepeace Thackeray
Mary Rowlandson	Sarah Bernhardt	William W. Walter
M. Wollstonecraft Shelley	Sarah C. Hallowell	William Shakespeare
Maud Lindsay	Selma Lagerlof	Winston Churchill
Max Beerbohm	Sherwood Anderson	Yei Theodora Ozaki
Myra Kelly	Sigmund Freud	Yogi Ramacharaka
Nathaniel Hawthrone	Standish O'Grady	Young E. Allison
Nicolo Machiavelli	Stanley Weyman	Zane Grey
O. F. Walton	Stella Benson	
Oscar Wilde	Stella M. Francis